Startup Learning, PBC
A public benefit corporation
www.LearnToReadOnline.org
info@LearnToReadOnline.org

Copyright ©2020 Startup Learning

All rights reserved. No part of this book may be reproduced in any form, including, but not limited to, storage in a retrieval system or transmission in any form or by any means, electronic, mechanical, photocopied, scanned, downloaded, recorded or otherwise without prior written permission.

ISBN 978-1-942696-06-3

Welcome to Startup Learning!

The **Intermediate Reading Course Book** is designed as a comprehensive Language Arts curriculum, which provides reading strategies for a solid foundation in literacy. Students will learn the necessary phonological awareness to read single and multi-syllable words, recognize vowel teams, and read short passages that build fluency and comprehension. The objective is for students to expand their vocabulary, comprehension skills, and become independent readers.

The Intermediate Reading curriculum addresses consonant digraphs, beginning consonant blends, vowel teams with multiple pronunciations, strategies for dividing words into syllables, as well as a variety of interactive spelling activities. The writing component includes learning to recognize and spell sight words, evaluate stories, answer questions in complete sentences, and practice writing basic descriptive, narrative, and compare-contrast paragraphs.

The lessons in the course book are aligned with the Common Core State Standards. Because text complexity plays an important role in students' reading progress, we use the Lexile reading levels to determine the complexity of each passage. The Lexile ranges for second and third grade are 450 - 790L.

It is our pleasure to have the opportunity to provide your child with a positive, successful, and rewarding experience in reading.

Sincerely,

Vivian Mendoza
Director, Literacy Curriculum

Contributors to the Course Book

Donna Davies

Vivian Mendoza

Bill Haff
Graphic Designer

Ben Kuyper
Cover Designer

Table of Contents

Overview i
Table of Contents iii

Course Book

Letter Names 1
Letter Sounds 2
Vowels and the Reading Code 3
Lesson 1: Consonant Digraphs 5
Lesson 2: Beginning Consonant Blends 11
Lesson 3: Vowel Teams: *al, er, ew* 19
Lesson 4: Vowel Teams: *ar, ir, ur, ay* 35
Lesson 5: Vowel Teams: *igh, oo, or, oi* 49
Lesson 6: Vowel Teams: *y, le, c with e, i, y* 61
Lesson 7: Vowel Teams: *oy, ol, ow, soft g* 75
Lesson 8: Vowel Teams: *cial, tial, au, wa* 89
Lesson 9: Vowel Teams: *ie, tur, soft g* 101
Lesson 10: Vowel Teams: *ear, dg, oo, ea* 115
Lesson 11: Vowel Teams: *ea, ey, sch, ear* 127
Lesson 12: Vowel Teams: *aw, ough, schwa o, ei* 141
Lesson 13: Vowel Teams: *ou, ow, schwa a* 153
Lesson 14: Vowel Teams: *tion, sion, ar* 169
Lesson 15: Vowel Teams: *or, ar, arr, er, err* 185

Skill Charts  **Student Version**

Letter Names - Job #1

Aa	Bb	Cc
Dd	Ee	Ff
Gg	Hh	Ii
Jj	Kk	Ll
Mm	Nn	Oo
Pp	Qq	Rr
Ss	Tt	Uu
Vv	Ww	Xx
Yy	Zz	

Skill Charts — Student Version

Letter Sounds - Job #2

	/b^uh/	/k^h/
a*	b	c*

/d^uh/		/f^ff/
d	e*	f

/g^uh/	/h^uh/	
g*	h	i*

/j^uh/	/k^h/	/L^LL/
j	k	l

/m^mm/	/n^nn/	
m	n	o*

/p^uh/	/kw^uh/	/r^rr/
p	q	r

/s^ss/	/t^uh/	
s*	t	u*

/v^vv/	/w^uh/	/ks^ss/
v	w	-x

/y^uh/	/z^zz/	
y*	z	* indicates letters that make more than one sound

page 2 — Startup Learning

Skill Charts

Student Version

Vowels and the Reading Code

Long Vowels		Short Vowels	
a-with-a-vowel-after says: 	 **acorn**	a-without-a-vowel-after says: 	 **apple**
e-with-a-vowel-after says:	 **eagle**	e-without-a-vowel-after says: 	 **egg**
i-with-a-vowel-after says:	 **ice cream**	i-without-a-vowel-after says:	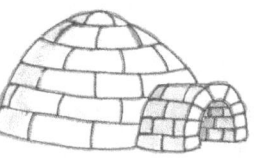 **igloo**
o-with-a-vowel-after says:	 **oboe**	o-without-a-vowel-after says: 	 **ox**
u-with-a-vowel-after says:	 **unicorn**	u-without-a-vowel-after says: 	 **umbrella**

Intermediate Reading

Lesson 1

Reading Lesson 1 — Student Version

Consonant Digraph Sounds

sh	 sheep	 shell	 ship
wh	 whale	 wheat	 wheel
ch	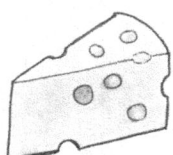 cheese	 lunch	 coach
th	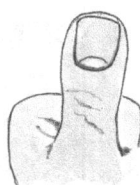 thumb	 path	 three
ph	 phone	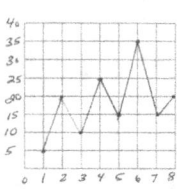 graph	 dolphin
qu	 queen	 quail	 quilt

Reading Lesson 1   Student Version

Reading Code Prompts

cheek

	Teacher says:	Student answers:
1)	What is the 1st vowel you can find in the word?	"e"
2)	Is [e] with-a-vowel-after, or [e] without?	"e" with
3)	Touch each letter and say the CODE.	/ch/ /ē/ /e/ /k/
4)	[e] with a vowel after says [ē].	
5)	Blend the sounds and read the word.	cheek

How to Read Short Vowel Words

check

	Teacher says:	Student answers:
1)	What is the 1st vowel you can find in the word?	"e"
2)	Is [e] with-a-vowel-after, or [e] without?	"e" without
3)	Touch each letter and say the CODE.	/ch/ /ĕ/ /k/
4)	[e] without says [ĕ].	
5)	Blend the sounds and read the word.	check

Intermediate Reading

Reading Lesson 1
Student Version

A. Consonant Digraphs

Directions:

1) Highlight or underline the consonant digraph.
2) Say the CODE and read the words.

sh

example: <u>sh</u>ell
shop
shade
rush
shake
fish

wh

example: <u>wh</u>eel
while
which
white
whisk
whiff

ch

example: <u>ch</u>ick
chin
chose
cheap
each
bench

th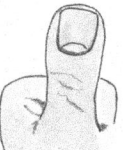

example: <u>th</u>umb
faith
paths
then
those
tenth

ph

example: <u>ph</u>one
phase
graph

qu

example: <u>qu</u>ilt
queen
quick
quite
quit
squeak

page 8

Startup Learning

Reading Lesson 1   Student Version

A. Consonant Digraphs

Directions: Fill in each blank using the best word from the three given choices.

example:
1) The tank was full of **fish**. chip sheep fish

2) Is the _____ white? cheese quit tenth

3) Her pink bike has big _____. shop wheels things

4) My dad went into the _____. phone shed thumb

5) Some old floors _____. queen chin squeak

6) Please take a _____ of that. photo bench snake

7) This is the _____ lap. whisk cash tenth

8) Most ducks usually _____. quack white each

Intermediate Reading

Reading Lesson 1

Student Version

B. Spelling Practice

"i" as in "ship"

Draw a ship in the box. Then write each word that the teacher says.

"a-e" as in "shape"

Draw your favorite shape in the box. Then write each word that the teacher says.

Super Challenge

Lesson 2

Reading Lesson 2

Student Version

Beginning Consonant Blend Sounds

bl		block	gl		globe
br		branch	gr		grapes
cl		clock	pl		plane
cr		crayons	pr		prize
dr		dragon	sc		scale
dw		dwelling	sk		skate
fl		flag	sl		slide
fr		fruit	sm		smile

page 12

Startup Learning

Reading Lesson 2 — Student Version

Beginning Consonant Blend Sounds

sn		snowman	spr		spring
sp		spade	str		string
st		stamp	phr	Way to go!	phrase
sw		swan	shr		shrimp
tr		tree	thr	3	three
tw		twins	squ		squid
scr		screen	k̶n*		knot
spl		splits	w̶r*		wren

*Super Challenge

Intermediate Reading — page 13

Reading Lesson 2

A. Consonant Blends

Directions:

1) Highlight or underline the consonant blend.
2) Say the CODE and read the words.

st

example: <u>st</u>ones
stop
steep
still
steam

str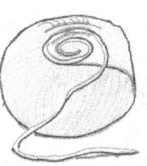

example: <u>str</u>ing
strain
stream
stripe

sc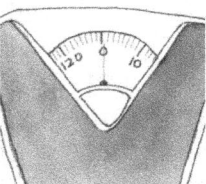

example: <u>sc</u>ale
scope
scan
score

scr

example: <u>scr</u>een
scrapes
scrub
scratch
script

sp

example: <u>sp</u>ade
Spain
spell
spear
spoke

spr

example: <u>spr</u>ing
sprain
sprint

Reading Lesson 2   Student Version

A. Consonant Blends

Directions:

1) Highlight or underline the consonant blend.
2) Say the CODE and read the words.

spl    kn 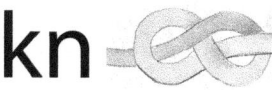   wr

example: <u>sp</u>lit   example: <s>k</s>not   example: <s>w</s>ren
splash   knee   wrap
splint   knead   write
spleen   knit   wrist
                 knob   wreath

Have students cross out the "k." It's silent.   Have students cross out the "w." It's silent.

Directions: Fill in each blank using the best word from the three given choices.

example:

1) Jerry skipped **stones** in the stream.   **knots stones spears**

2) My friend broke her _____ .   **wrist knob scrape**

3) The train came to a _____ .   **wreath stream stop**

4) Grandma can _____ a scarf.   **split knit scratch**

Intermediate Reading   page 15

Reading Lesson 2

B. Beginning Consonant Blend Sounds

Directions: Fill in each blank using the best word from the three given choices.

example:

1) The fishers caught **shrimp** . flag smile shrimp

2) That is the tallest _____ . bread tree fruit

3) Please put the fish on the _____ . scrape scale bake

4) The _____ is 10 minutes fast. grapes gloves clock

5) Where are the _____ ? squish twins slim

6) Use _____ to draw that. crayons planes skunks

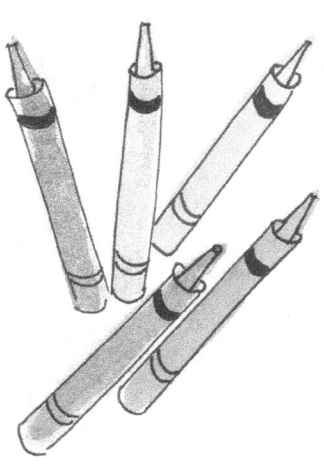

Reading Lesson 2 — Student Version

C. Spelling Practice

"oa" as in "boat"

Draw a boat in the box. Then write each word that the teacher says.

"ai" as in "rain"

Write the number four in the box. Then write each word that the teacher says.

Super Challenge

Reading Lesson 2

Student Version

C. Spelling Practice

"ee" as in "tree"

Draw a tree in the box. Then write each word that the teacher says.

"ea" as in "treat"

Draw your favorite treat in the box. Then write each word that the teacher says.

Super Challenge

page 18

Startup Learning

Lesson 3

Reading Lesson 3

A. Vowel Teams

Directions: Highlight the vowel team and read each word.

"al" says /awl/ as in "waterfall"

palm	salt	tall	mall
small	stall	hall	calm
ball	wall	call	bald

"er" says /r/ as in "feather"

her	perch	herd	clerk
fern	perm	term	perk
whisper	sweeter	hamster	smaller

"ew" says /oo/ as in "jewel"

knew	stew	grew	blew
dew	threw	flew	crew
drew	chew	new	few

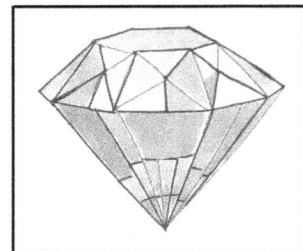

Reading Lesson 3   Student Version

A. Vowel Teams

Directions: Highlight or underline the "ed," draw a box around the consonant before "ed," and read each word.

1) "Ed" is pronounced |ĕd| if the end of the word sounds like |t| or |d|.

Example: The old house was haunted.

    wanted   rested   added

2) "Ed" is pronounced |t| if the end of the word sounds like |p|, |k|, |s|, |ch|, |sh|, or |th|.

Example: I helped my older sister make cookies.

    stopped   parked   watched

3) "Ed" is pronounced |d^{uh}| for all other ending sounds like |a|, |b|, |e|, |g|, |h|, |i|, |j|, |l|, |m|, |n|, |o|, |q|, |r|, |u|, |v|, |w|, |x|, |y|, or |z|.

Example: Cameron played soccer this afternoon.

    pulled   seemed   covered

Directions: Read the following sentences, underline the "ed," and match the ending sound - |t|, |d^{uh}|, or |ĕd|.

1. The car suddenly stopped. | t |

2. I really wanted to go to the beach. | d^{uh} |

3. The hills were covered with snow. | ĕd |

Intermediate Reading

Reading Lesson 3

Student Version

B. Spelling Practice

Directions: First, highlight the vowel team in each word. Next, write these words in the correct vowel section.

Word List - New Vowel Teams
1. soc<u>er</u> ✓
2. c<u>a</u>lm ✓
3. kn<u>ew</u> ✓
4. salt
5. threw
6. chew
7. herself
8. pitcher
9. small

"al" often says /awl/ as in "waterfall"

example: c<u>a</u>lm

"ew" says /oo/ as in "jewel"

example: kn<u>ew</u>

"er" says /r/ as in "feather"

example: soc<u>er</u>

page 22

Startup Learning

Reading Lesson 3 — Student Version

C. Decoding Practice

**There are four strategies that help us divide words into syllables.
Every syllable must have a vowel.**

Strategy 1:
Dividing Words Into Syllables - Double-same/double-different consonants

Find the two middle consonants and mark a "syllable wall" inside them.
Make sure there is a vowel on either side of the syllable wall.

Example 1 - Double-same	Example 2 - Double-different
suf|fix	ad|mit

runner   tablet
summer   winter
committee   perfect

Strategy 2:
Dividing Words Into Syllables - Open/closed syllables

When two consonants are not in the middle of a word, do the following:

1) Find the first vowel and put a syllable wall after it. The vowel will say its name. **This is an example of an open syllable.**

2) Make a CVC pattern (Consonant-Vowel-Consonant) and put a syllable wall after it. The vowel will make a short vowel sound. **This is an example of a closed syllable.** (the CVC pattern is highlighted in the example)

Example 1 - Open Syllables	Example 2 - Closed Syllables
si|lent	lem|on (cvc)

paper   limit
tiger   rapid
relax   finish

Intermediate Reading

Reading Lesson 3   Student Version

C. Decoding Practice

Strategy 3: Compound Words

Formed when two small words are put together to make one new big word.

Directions: Draw a line between these words to make compound words.

bed	side
pan	time
sun	set
in	cake

Directions: Circle the two words that make up each compound word.

1. s a n d b o x
2. m i l k s h a k e
3. c u p c a k e
4. n i c k n a m e

Directions: Use the words in the box to form compound words with "ball" and "back."

| soft | pack | base | stage |
| foot | ground | basket | track |

ball   **back**

_____ ball   back _____

_____ ball   back _____

_____ ball   back _____

_____ ball   back _____

Reading Lesson 3 — Student Version

C. Decoding Practice

Strategy 4: Prefixes and Suffixes

A prefix is a word part added to the beginning of a base word. Adding a prefix changes the meaning of a word.

Directions:
Draw a line to match each word to its meaning.

Prefix	Meaning
unkind	pay before
repaint	paint again
misplace	not kind
prepay	put in the wrong place

> un means "not"
> pre means "before"
> mis means "wrong"
> re means "again"

Directions: Use the word bank to fill in the blanks.

unsafe	preheat	misspell	redo

example:
1) My sister had lost her homework, and she had to _____redo_____ it.

2) Grandma forgot to _____ the oven.

3) I practiced new words so I did not _____ them.

4) It's _____ for your little sister to go down the stairs alone.

Reading Lesson 3

D. Sight Words

Directions: Choose the right word from the box and write it in the sentence.

going	everyone	from
could		have

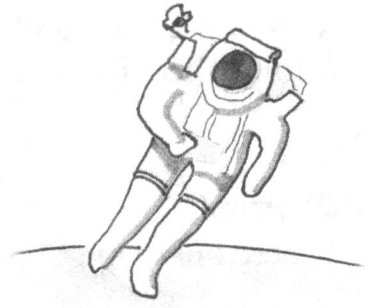

example:

1) **Everyone** was on the rocketship.

2) They were _____ the U.S.A.

3) They _____ see the planet.

4) They were _____ to Mars.

5) "Do you _____ gear ready?"

E. Vocabulary

Directions: Read each new word and meaning.

alert: being watchful, be ready to act quickly

focus: pay attention to a center of interest

mitt: a baseball catcher's glove

pitcher: in baseball, the person throwing the ball to the batter

Reading Lesson 3   Student Version

F. Cloze Reading

Directions: Fill in the blank spaces with the right words from the box.

| perfect | stepped | swung | herself |
| everyone | pitcher | mitt | alert |

The Amazing Catch

The bases were loaded on this **perfect** summer day.

Emily, the smallest and newest person on her team was near second base. Just then, a kid nicknamed Nate _____ up to bat. Everyone knew he was the best hitter on his team.

Emily became _____ and punched the palm of her mitt. All her team focused on home plate. The _____ threw the ball. Nate _____ his bat. The ball flew fast to Emily. Could she catch the ball?

"I can do this" she said to _____.

Rising on her toes, Emily lifted up her _____ and grabbed the ball. Nate was out! _____ chanted her name.

Intermediate Reading   page 27

Reading Lesson 3   Student Version

G. Written Response

Directions: Read each question, cross out the asking word (who/what/when/where) and use the remaining words to write a complete answer.

Example: Who is the newest person on the team?

Emily is the newest person on the team.

1) Who was the best hitter on the other team?

2) Were the bases loaded?

3) Who caught Nate's fly ball?

Reading Lesson 3   Student Version

H. Vowel Sound Practice

The "al" sound. Read these words with the "al" spelling.
Then draw a picture for each in the empty box.

baseball   waterfall   palm tree

The "er" sound. Write "er" to complete each word.
Then write the whole word in the empty space.

riv

lett

ov

sist

The "ew" sound. Draw a circle around the words with the "ew" pattern.

| renew | hilltop | marvel | mildew | chewy |
| barking | pardon | fewer | pesky | silent |

Intermediate Reading

Reading Lesson 3
Student Version

I. Spelling Practice

"al" as in "ball"
Draw a ball in the box. Then write three words with "al" in them.

"er" as in "fern"
Draw a fern in the box. Then write three words with "er" in them.

"ew" as in "flew"
Draw something that flew in the box. Then write three words with "ew" in them.

"ed" as in "sailed"
Draw something that sailed in the box. Then write three words with "ed" in them.

Reading Lesson 3 — Student Version

J. Super Sentences

A **super sentence** must have an article, adjective, noun, verb, and a *where* and *why*.

Directions: Using the chart below, write a super sentence in the space provided using only one entry from each column. It must make sense!

Article	Adjective	Noun	Verb	Where?	Why?
One	honest	clown	sat down	at the gate	to uncover a new clue.
The	sandy	pirate	hollered	in the grassland	to find the missing gold.
The	cheerful	cowgirl	raced around	at the market	to find a lost cow.
A	curious	detective	searched	on the sidewalk	to buy a brand new stove.
One	energetic	baker	stomped	in the store	to collect an audience.

Reading Lesson 3 — Student Version

J. Super Sentences

Make a basic sentence with a subject (noun) and predicate (verb).
Example: *My dog rolled over.* **Now it is your turn:**

Now add words that describe your subject.
Example: *My fluffy, big, white dog rolled over.*
Now it is your turn:

Now add a prepositional phrase that answers the question, *Where?*
Example: *My fluffy, big, white dog rolled over in the muddy water.*
Now it is your turn:

Finally, add a clause using the beginning word *before*, *after*, or *since*.
Example: *My fluffy, big, white dog rolled over in the muddy water after I gave her a bath.* A clause is a phrase - a few words together.
Now it is your turn:

Reading Lesson 3 — Student Version

K. Writing Interesting Sentences

Directions: Create a picture in your mind. Now, write it!

Example: I crossed the track. (dull)
The railroad track was straight and empty for miles and miles, so I crossed it. (more interesting)

1) The stars shine.

_____

_____

_____

In your sentences above:

- Circle the nouns with a red marker or crayon.
- Underline the verbs with a green marker or crayon.
- Underline the adjectives with a blue marker or crayon.
- Put parentheses ( ) around your clauses that answer the questions who, what, where, when, why.

Intermediate Reading — page 33

Lesson 4

Reading Lesson 4

A. Vowel Teams

Directions: Highlight the vowel team and read each word.

"ar" says /är/ as in "garden"

shark	start	mark	park
harp	hard	dark	part
March	farmer	market	partner

"ir" says /er/ as in "songbird"

chirp	whirl	firm	stir
skirt	dirt	first	shirt
twirl	thirty	squirrel	birthday

"ur" says /er/ as in "purse"

burst	curve	fur	surf
turn	blur	curb	blurt
nursery	spurt	turkey	surprise

"ay" says /long a/ as in "crayons"

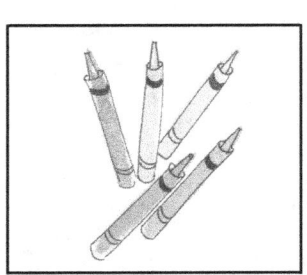

clay	play	way	spray
day	tray	stay	relay
subway	fairway	stairway	playpen

Reading Lesson 4   Student Version

B. Spelling Practice

Directions: First, highlight the vowel team in each word.
Next, write these words in the correct vowel section.

Word List - New Vowel Teams

1. c<u>ar</u> ✓
2. st<u>ir</u> ✓
3. p<u>ur</u>ple ✓
4. d<u>ay</u> ✓
5. nursery
6. swirl
7. shirt
8. scarf
9. hamburger
10. harm
11. holiday
12. spray

"ar" says /är/ as in "garden"

example: c<u>ar</u>

"ir" says /er/ as in "bird"

example: st<u>ir</u>

"ur" says /er/ as in "purse"

example: p<u>ur</u>ple

"ay" says /long a/ as in "crayon"

example: d<u>ay</u>

Intermediate Reading

Reading Lesson 4

C. Decoding Practice

There are four strategies that help us divide words into syllables. Every syllable must have a vowel.

Strategy 1:
Dividing Words Into Syllables - Double-same/double-different consonants

Find the two middle consonants and mark a "syllable wall" inside them. Make sure there is a vowel on either side of the syllable wall.

Example 1 - Double-same	**Example 2 - Double-different**
suf|fix	ad|mit

lesson	thunder
letter	number
rabbit	mildew

Strategy 2:
Dividing Words Into Syllables - Open/closed syllables

When two consonants are not in the middle of a word, do the following:

1) Find the first vowel and put a syllable wall after it. The vowel will say its name. **This is an example of an open syllable.**

2) Make a CVC pattern (Consonant-Vowel-Consonant) and put a syllable wall after it. The vowel will make a short vowel sound. **This is an example of a closed syllable.** (the CVC pattern is highlighted in the example)

Example 1 - Open Syllables	**Example 2 - Closed Syllables**
si|lent	CVC lem|on

tiger	river
broken	cabin
music	seven

Reading Lesson 4 — Student Version

C. Decoding Practice

Strategy 3: Compound Words

Formed when two small words are put together to make one new big word.

Directions: Draw a line between these words to make compound words.

pig	time
sail	pen
bed	boat
chop	stick

Directions: Circle the two words that make up each compound word.

1. flagpole
2. pineapple
3. catfish
4. teaspoon

Directions: Use the words in the box to form compound words with "day" and "water."

mark	dream	light	fall
front	wheel	birth	week

<u>day</u>   <u>water</u>

day _____   water _____

_____ day   water _____

day _____   water _____

_____ day   water _____

Reading Lesson 4

Student Version

C. Decoding Practice

Strategy 4: Prefixes and Suffixes

A suffix is a word part added to the end of a base word. Adding a suffix changes the meaning of a word.

Directions:
Draw a line to match each word to its meaning.

suffix	Meaning
twirled	without care
cheerful	twirl in the past
careless	full of cheer

> ed = past tense
> ful means "full of"
> less means "without"

Directions: Use the word bank to fill in the blanks.

| useful | hairless | decorated | barked |

example:
1) The bald eagle is **hairless**.

2) Irma's birthday cake was beautifully _____.

3) The pen is a _____ writing tool.

4) The hungry dog _____ all night.

Reading Lesson 4

Student Version

D. Sight Words

Directions: Choose the right word from the box and write it in the sentence.

there	here	said
other	when	they

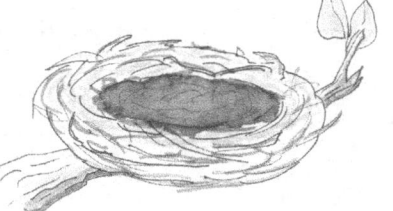

example:

1) **They** _____ went shopping at the mall.

2) They got lost driving _____.

3) Can you return the _____ magazine?

4) The hungry cat _____ "meow."

5) We can play _____ you finish your homework.

6) The bluebird made a nest _____ in my backyard.

E. Vocabulary

Directions: Read each new word and meaning.

suddenly: happens unexpectedly in a short amount of time

giggle: to laugh with repeated, short, high sounds

ribbon: a narrow strip of colorful silk-like fabric

twirl: to turn around very fast

Reading Lesson 4

F. Cloze Reading

<u>Directions</u>: **Fill in the blank spaces with the right words from the box.**

| birthday | children | giggled | purred |
| games | arrive | kitten | ribbon |

The Big Surprise

It was the third Saturday in March when Irma had her birthday party.

All the children she invited started to _____arrive_____. First they

blew bubbles. They _____ when they burst. Then the

_____ marched and twirled to music. Irma opened

presents and they ate a birthday cake. Just before they played

_____ in the park, Irma suddenly heard a small "meow."

She went in the hallway and saw a big surprise.

There in a box with a pretty _____ on it was a kitten gazing

up at her. Irma was amazed because she wanted a _____ so

much! His fur was soft and he _____

when she held him. This was the best

_____ gift ever!

Reading Lesson 4　　　　　　　　　Student Version

G. Written Response

Directions: Read each question, cross out the asking word (who/what/when/where) and use the remaining words to write a complete answer.

Example: Who had a birthday party?

> Irma had a birthday party.

1) Who played games in the park?

2) What was Irma's big surprise?

3) What was the kitten in?

Reading Lesson 4

Student Version

H. Vowel Sound Practice

The "ar" sound. Read these "ar" words, then draw a picture for each in the empty box.

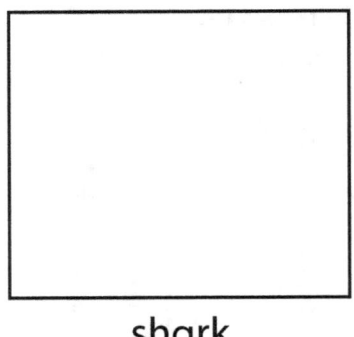

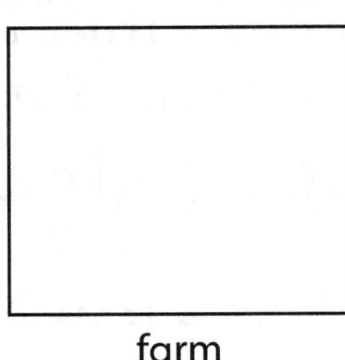

shark　　　　　　　garden　　　　　　　farm

The "ir" sound. Write "ir" to complete each word, then write the word in the empty space.

wh___l　　　　　　　　　　ch___p

squ___rel　　　　　　　　　st___

The "ur" sound. Draw a circle around the words with the "ur" pattern.

nursery	partner	hunting	spurt	prize
lizard	purses	enchanted	current	hallway

The "ay" sound. Read these "ay" words, then draw a picture for each in the empty box.

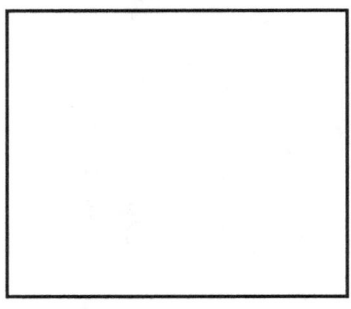
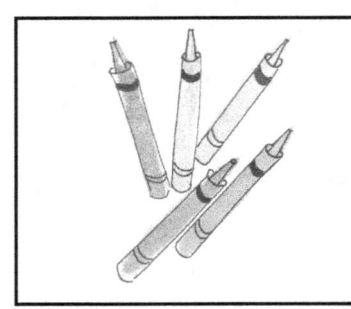
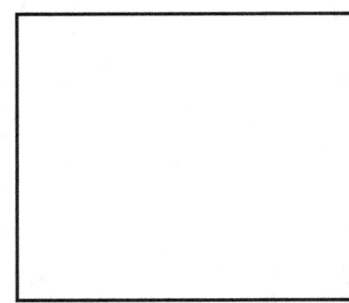

stairway　　　　　　　crayon　　　　　　　archway

Reading Lesson 4

Student Version

I. Spelling Practice

"ar" as in "car"
Draw a car in the box. Then write three words with "ar" in them.

"ir" as in "shirt"
Draw a shirt in the box. Then write three words with "ir" in them.

"ur" as in "turtle"
Draw a turtle in the box. Then write three words with "ur" in them.

"ay" as in "play"
Draw a play in the box. Then write three words with "ay" in them.

Intermediate Reading

page 45

Reading Lesson 4   Student Version

J. Basic Paragraphs

Directions:
1. Read the paragraph below about mailing a letter.
2. Underline the topic sentence in green.
3. Underline the supporting sentences in yellow.
4. Underline the concluding sentence in green.

Mailing a letter is pretty easy to do.

First, you stuff the letter into an envelope.

Next, you write the address on the front and stick on a stamp.

Last, you put it in a mailbox or take it to the post office.

I really like getting cards and letters so I make sure I send some, too!

Reading Lesson 4 — Student Version

K. Supporting Sentences

Directions: Read the topic sentence and then write two supporting details.

Topic sentence:
Picking up and putting away my toys is a task I need to do quite often.

First, I _____
_____

Then, I _____
_____

Concluding sentence:
I really like to see my room so neat and orderly.

Lesson 5

Reading Lesson 5

A. Vowel Teams

Directions: Highlight the vowel team and read each word.

"igh" says /long i/ as in "night"

light	flight	tight	right
sight	bright	might	high
flashlight	twilight	midnight	daylight

"oo" says /oo/ as in "zoo"

soon	pool	loose	boot
food	cool	tool	moon
school	smooth	scoops	balloon

"or" says /or/ as in "acorn"

storm	born	morning	corn
short	before	horn	shore
organ	perform	explore	forest

"oi" says /oi/ as in "coin"

soil	boil	spoil	toil
join	broil	oil	coil
asteroid	moist	point	noise

Reading Lesson 5 Student Version

B. Spelling Practice

Directions: First, highlight the vowel team in each word. Next, write these words in the correct vowel section.

Word List - New Vowel Teams

1. br<u>igh</u>t ✓
2. c<u>oo</u>l ✓
3. f<u>or</u>k ✓
4. p<u>oi</u>nt ✓
5. thorns
6. daylight
7. choose
8. scoop
9. tonight
10. disappoint
11. stormed
12. moist

"igh" says /ī/ as in "night"

example: br<u>igh</u>t

"oo" says /oo/ as in "zoo"

example: c<u>oo</u>l

"or" says /or/ as in "acorn"

example: f<u>or</u>k

"oi" says /oi/ as in "coin"

example: p<u>oi</u>nt

Reading Lesson 5 — Student Version

C. Decoding Practice

There are four strategies that help us divide words into syllables. Every syllable must have a vowel.

Strategy 1:
Dividing Words Into Syllables - Double-same/double-different consonants

Find the two middle consonants and mark a "syllable wall" inside them. Make sure there is a vowel on either side of the syllable wall.

<u>Example 1</u> - Double-same	<u>Example 2</u> - Double-different
suf|fix	ad|mit

jello   market
shopping   corner
ladder   export

Strategy 2:
Dividing Words Into Syllables - Open/closed syllables

When two consonants are not in the middle of a word, do the following:

1) Find the first vowel and put a syllable wall after it. The vowel will say its name. **This is an example of an open syllable.**

2) Make a CVC pattern (Consonant-Vowel-Consonant) and put a syllable wall after it. The vowel will make a short vowel sound. **This is an example of a closed syllable.** (the CVC pattern is highlighted in the example)

<u>Example 1</u> - Open Syllables	<u>Example 2</u> - Closed Syllables
si|lent	l e m|o n (CVC)

gravy   comet
hotel   topic
meter   visit

Reading Lesson 5   Student Version

C. Decoding Practice

Strategy 3: Compound Words

Formed when two small words are put together to make one new big word.

Directions: Draw a line between these words to make compound words.

arm	book
candy	chair
corn	dog
cook	cane

Directions: Circle the two words that make up each compound word.

1. flashlight
2. fishnet
3. doorbell
4. spacecraft

Directions: Use the words in the box to form compound words with "night" and "door."

shift	step	mid	knob
mare	mat	bell	time

<u>night</u>   <u>door</u>

night _____   door _____

night _____   door _____

_____ night   door _____

night _____   door _____

Intermediate Reading   page 53

Reading Lesson 5

Student Version

C. Decoding Practice

Directions: Add a base word from the word bank to each house. Add the prefix or suffix that's in the house, then write the newly formed word underneath the house.

| install | toast | help |
| fear | pay | connect |

Example:

1)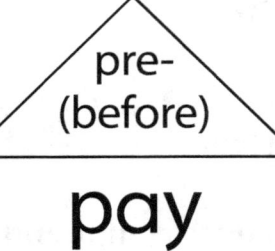

prepay

2)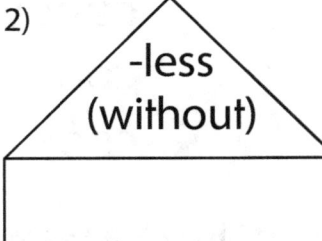

3)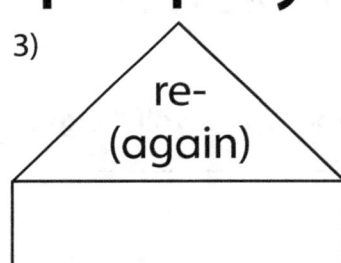

4)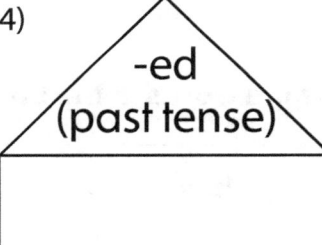

5)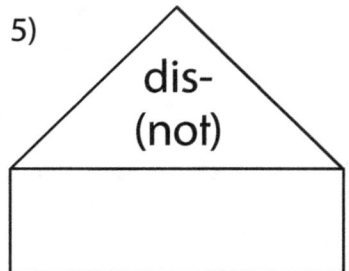

6)

page 54 — Startup Learning

Reading Lesson 5   Student Version

D. Sight Words

Directions: Choose the right word from the box and write it in the sentence.

what	those	off
where	any	into

example:
1) Niki skated so fast she skated **off** the ice.

2) Miles didn't eat _____ of the fresh, hot cookies.

3) Could you please hand me _____ Legos?

4) Hannah did not know _____ to go shopping.

5) We have to wait to get _____ the theater.

6) Do you know _____ books you are getting?

E. Vocabulary

Directions: Read each new word and meaning.

meteor: rocks in the solar system

asteroid: small rocky body that orbits the sun

landscape: the land that can be seen in one glance

crater: a hole made by the impact of a meteor or asteroid

Reading Lesson 5   Student Version

F. Cloze Reading

Directions: Fill in the blank spaces with the right words from the box.

| erupt | might | lava | storms | moon |
| bright | cooled | crater | see | |

The Man in the Moon

Have you seen "The Man in the Moon?" What seems to be a face is part of the moon's landscape. There isn't any air on the moon so meteors and asteroids don't burn up. Those great big rocks crash into the **moon** creating vast craters.

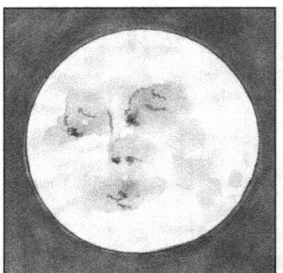

There isn't any wind or rain or _____ on the moon to erode the soil or craters. So we can still _____ the high, pointed _____ walls when the _____ sunlight jumps off the moon and back to us.

Volcanos used to _____ on the moon. The dark patches are spots where hot dark _____ pooled. Soon it _____ into hard, smooth rock. The craters and dark lava areas make up the face. You _____ see "The Man in the Moon." It is a playful sight!

page 56   Startup Learning

Reading Lesson 5   Student Version

G. Written Response

Directions: Read each question and answer with a complete sentence.

1) What crashes into the moon?

2) Is there wind on the moon?

3) Is there any rain on the moon?

Reading Lesson 5

H. Vowel Sound Practice

The "igh" sound. Read these "igh" words, then draw a picture for each in the empty box.

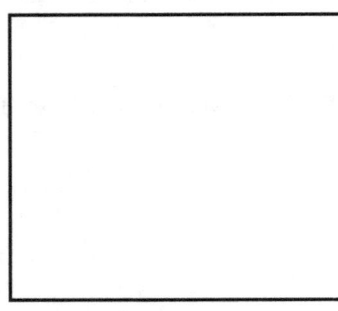

flashlight   night   flight

The "oo" sound. Write "oo" to complete each word, then write the word in the empty space.

r___t   sp___n

ball___n   sch___l

The "oi" sound. Draw a circle around the words with the "oi" pattern.

subway	oils	hunt	prints	jump
avoid	sand	moist	stamp	foil

The "or" sound. Read these "or" words, then draw a picture for each in the empty box.

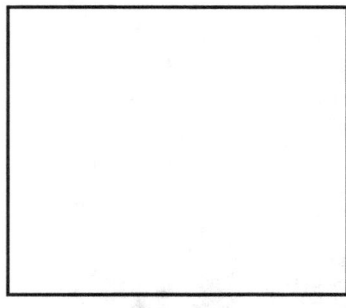

horn   popcorn   storm

Reading Lesson 5 — Student Version

I. Spelling Practice

"igh" as in "spotlight"
Draw a spotlight in the box. Then write three words with "igh" in them.

"oo" as in "school"
Write three words with "oo" in them.

"or" as in "acorn"
Write three words with "or" in them.

"oi" as in "coil"
Draw a coil in the box. Then write three words with "oi" in them.

Reading Lesson 5   Student Version

J. Combine Two Ideas in One Sentence

Directions: Linking words connect two thoughts. Link each set of two sentences below using the best linking word, either *and*, *or*, or *so*.

Example: Ling went to the zoo. Ling saw a zebra there. (use *and*, *or*, or *so*)

Ling went to the zoo and saw a zebra there.

1) Sparky is my cute kitty. Sparky loves to play with yarn. (use *and*, *or*, or *so*)

2) Alicia goes to the library. She can study there. (use *and*, *or*, or *so*)

3) Do you like peaches? Do you like pears? (use *and*, *or*, or *so*)

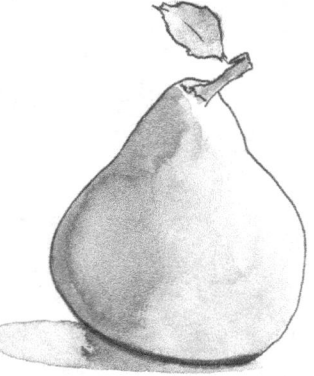

Lesson 6

Reading Lesson 6

A. Vowel Teams

<u>Directions</u>: Highlight the vowel team and read each word.

"<u>y</u>" says /e/ as in "pupp<u>y</u>" at the end of a word with two or more syllables

funny	silly	easy	family
candy	tasty	ready	party
speedy	kitty	misty	tangy

"<u>le</u>" says /l/ as in "cast<u>le</u>" at the end of a word with two or more syllables

candle	wiggle	apple	cradle
able	simple	little	bubble
stable	settle	possible	middle

"<u>c</u>" says /s/ as in "fa<u>c</u>e" when an "e" or "i" or "y" follows it

cent	dance	fence	applesauce
fancy	success	cider	processor
piece	place	spicy	cinnamon

Reading Lesson 6   Student Version

B. Spelling Practice

Directions: First, highlight the vowel team in each word. Next, write these words in the correct vowel section.

Word List - New Vowel Teams

1. mist<u>y</u> ✓
2. midd<u>le</u> ✓
3. pla<u>c</u>e ✓
4. windy
5. sample
6. crumble
7. cycle
8. hurry
9. dice

"y" says /e/ as in "puppy"

example: mist<u>y</u>

"le" says /l/ as in "castle"

example: midd<u>le</u>

"c" says /s/ if it is followed by "e," "i," or "y"

example: pla<u>c</u>e

Intermediate Reading

Reading Lesson 6

C. Decoding Practice

**There are four strategies that help us divide words into syllables.
Every syllable must have a vowel.**

Strategy 1:
Dividing Words Into Syllables - Double-same/double-different consonants

Find the two middle consonants and mark a "syllable wall" inside them.
Make sure there is a vowel on either side of the syllable wall.

Example 1 - Double-same	Example 2 - Double-different
suf|fix	ad|mit

puzzle	velvet
middle	party
funny	fancy

Strategy 2:
Dividing Words Into Syllables - Open/closed syllables

When two consonants are not in the middle of a word, do the following:

1) Find the first vowel and put a syllable wall after it. The vowel will say its name. **This is an example of an open syllable.**

2) Make a CVC pattern (Consonant-Vowel-Consonant) and put a syllable wall after it. The vowel will make a short vowel sound. **This is an example of a closed syllable.** (the CVC pattern is highlighted in the example)

Example 1 - Open Syllables	Example 2 - Closed Syllables
si|lent	lem|on (cvc)

title	comics
staple	model
clover	tropic

Reading Lesson 6 — Student Version

C. Decoding Practice

Strategy 3: <u>Compound Words</u>

Formed when two small words are put together to make one new big word.

<u>Directions</u>: Draw a line between these words to make compound words.

fire	less
egg	mint
end	cracker
pepper	nog

<u>Directions</u>: Circle the two words that make up each compound word.

1. j e l l y f i s h   3. s e v e n t e e n
2. t e l e s c o p e   4. b u t t e r f l y

<u>Directions</u>: Use words in the box to form compound words with "mail" and "down."

stream	box	town	load
hill	man	air	bag

<u>**mail**</u>   <u>**down**</u>

mail _____   down _____

mail _____   down _____

_____ mail   down _____

mail _____   down _____

Reading Lesson 6

Student Version

C. Decoding Practice

Strategy 4: Prefixes and Suffixes

A prefix is a word part added to the beginning of a base word. Adding a prefix changes the meaning of a word.

> <u>over</u> means "extra"
> <u>dis</u> means "not"
> <u>im</u> means "not"
> <u>ex</u> means "out"

Directions:
Draw a line to match each word to its meaning.

Prefix	Meaning
overtime	to be out of date
distract	extra time
expire	not paying attention
impossible	unable to happen

Directions: Use the word bank to fill in the blanks.

overtime	exports	impatient	dislike

example:
1) My dad often has to work **overtime**.

2) Is there any type of candy that you _____?

3) The driver was very _____ because he was running late.

4) Costa Rica _____ bananas to other countries.

Reading Lesson 6   Student Version

D. Sight Words

Directions: Choose the right word from the box and write it in the sentence.

but	had	them
of	then	that

example:
1) As she loved chickens, Helen took good care of **them**.

2) Keenan liked them, too, _____ he didn't like the work.

3) _____ all the hens, Mable was the smallest.

4) She laid eggs _____ were speckled.

5) The baby chicks _____ a warm place to live.

6) When they grew big, _____ they were sold.

E. Vocabulary

Directions: Read each new word and meaning.

processor: a machine with blades that cuts and blends food

pulp: the soft juicy, fleshy part of a fruit

cider: the juice pressed out of a fruit

cheesecloth: a thin, loosely woven cotton cloth

Intermediate Reading

Reading Lesson 6

Student Version

F. Cloze Reading

Directions: Fill in the blank spaces with the right words from the box.

smaller	Dice	pulp	Add
adults	green	glass	drink

Fresh Apple Cider

Have you ever had a glass of fresh apple cider? It is tangy! It is possible to make cider at home with help from **adults**. There are five simple steps. Start by washing many red or _____ apples. Then, remove the core from the apples. That means to cut away the center part. _____ each apple into quarters or _____ pieces.

Put the little pieces in a food processor or blender and swirl the apples. This step makes them look like applesauce. Push this _____ through a fine mesh strainer or squeeze the pulp through a piece of cheesecloth. Success!

Now, it is ready to _____. But you might want to make it spicy. _____ a little nutmeg or lemon peel or ginger to the cider in a _____. On a holiday, you could add cinnamon sticks for a fancy treat.

page 68

Startup Learning

Reading Lesson 6

Student Version

G. Written Response

Directions: Read each question and answer with a complete sentence.

1) Would you like to make apple cider?

2) What is the second step in the process?

3) What can you add to make the drink spicy?

Reading Lesson 6

H. Vowel Sound Practice

The "y" sound. Read these words with the "y" spelling.
Then draw a picture for each in the empty box.

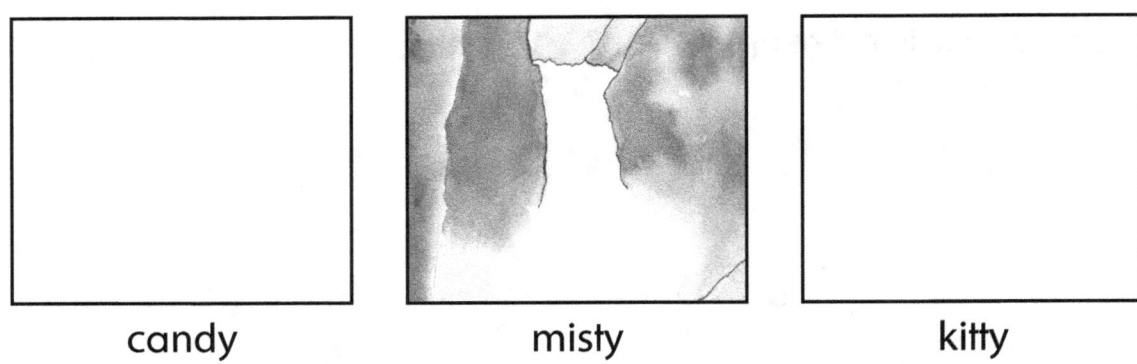

candy　　　　　misty　　　　　kitty

The "le" sound. Write "le" to complete each word.
Then write the whole word in the empty space.

example: circ **le**　　**circle**

bubb

wigg

crad

The soft "c" sound. Draw a circle around the words with the "c" pattern.

| battle | voice | family | tacky | circus |
| mince | space | feeble | tasty | embrace |

page 70

Reading Lesson 6

Student Version

I. Spelling Practice

"y" as in "family"
Draw a family in the box. Then write three words with "y" in them.

"le" as in "table"
Draw a table in the box. Then write three words with "le" in them.

"c" as in "ice cream"
Draw ice cream in the box. Then write three words with "c" in them.

Intermediate Reading

Reading Lesson 6

J. Write a Paragraph

Directions: Write sentences to support the topic sentence. Then highlight the transition words in yellow.

1) Every day, I help make and pack my lunch for school. This is how I do it:

First, I

Second, I

Last of all, I

By helping to make my lunch, I'm sure to get the food I like to eat.

Reading Lesson 6   Student Version

J. Write a Paragraph

Directions: Write sentences to support the topic sentence.
Then highlight the transition words in yellow.

2) Today was very special because it was the first day I went to a big zoo.

In the morning,

That afternoon,

Before we left the zoo,

But most of all, I enjoyed feeding a giraffe and watching his long tongue.

Intermediate Reading

Reading Lesson 6

Student Version

K. Punctuation

Directions: Add the correct punctuation,
choosing from a period (.), question mark (?), or exclamation point (!)
When you are done, act out this dialogue as a play! Take turns.

Parent: Would you like to learn how to sew___

Child: Yes, I would love to learn how to sew___

Parent: What is the first thing you would like to make___

Child: I would like to make an elephant costume___

Parent: That is too complicated for a first project___

Child: We are putting on a puppet show at school___

Child: I am one of the three bears___

Parent: Would you like to sew a bear puppet___

Child: Yes I would love to learn to sew on that project___

Parent: Then let's get started___

Lesson 7

Reading Lesson 7

A. Vowel Teams

Directions: Highlight the vowel team and read each word.

"oy" says /oi/ as in "toy"

boy	oyster	royal	loyal
voyage	decoy	annoy	cowboy
overjoyed	employ	destroy	Troy

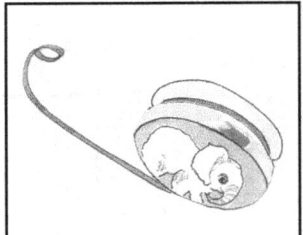

"ol" says /ol/ as in "oldest"

told	golden	sold	bold
hole	solar	fold	toll
bolted	troll	yolk	holding

"ow" says /o/ as in "snowman"

know	show	blow	own
below	glowed	snowy	pillow
rainbow	shallow	yellow	willow

"soft g" says /j/ as in "giraffe"

ginger	giant	apology	fragile
gentle	legend	danger	plunged
magically	allergy	urgently	suggest

Reading Lesson 7   Student Version

B. Spelling Practice

Directions: First, highlight the vowel group in each word.
Next, write these words in the correct vowel section.

Word List - New Vowel Teams

1. empl<u>oy</u> ✓
2. c<u>ol</u>der ✓
3. wind<u>ow</u> ✓
4. <u>g</u>entle ✓
5. overjoy
6. giant
7. oldest
8. fragile
9. goldfish
10. oyster
11. elbow
12. shallow

"oy" says /oi/ as in "toy"

example: empl<u>oy</u>

"ol" says /ol/ as in "oldest"

example: c<u>ol</u>der

"ow" says /o/ as in "snowman"

example: wind<u>ow</u>

"soft g" says /j/ as in "giraffe"

example: <u>g</u>entle

Intermediate Reading

Reading Lesson 7
Student Version

C. Decoding Practice

**There are four strategies that help us divide words into syllables.
Every syllable must have a vowel.**

Strategy 1:
Dividing Words Into Syllables - Double-same/double-different consonants

Find the two middle consonants and mark a "syllable wall" inside them. Make sure there is a vowel on either side of the syllable wall.

Example 1 - Double-same
suf|fix

Example 2 - Double-different
ad|mit

hobby   publish
kennel   chapter
ribbon   adverb

Strategy 2:
Dividing Words Into Syllables - Open/closed syllables

When two consonants are not in the middle of a word, do the following:

1) Find the first vowel and put a syllable wall after it. The vowel will say its name. **This is an example of an open syllable.**

2) Make a CVC pattern (Consonant-Vowel-Consonant) and put a syllable wall after it. The vowel will make a short vowel sound. **This is an example of a closed syllable.** (the CVC pattern is highlighted in the example)

Example 1 - Open Syllables
si|lent

Example 2 - Closed Syllables
c v c
lem|on

defend   hockey
protect   wagon
erase   chisel

Reading Lesson 7	Student Version

C. Decoding Practice

Strategy 3: Compound Words

Formed when two small words are put together to make one new big word.

Directions: Draw a line between these words to make compound words.

home	tail
pea	brush
pony	nut
tooth	work

Directions: Circle the two words that make up each compound word.

1. g i n g e r b r e a d
2. c o w b o y
3. s n o w f l a k e
4. w i l d c a t

Directions: Use the words in the box to form compound words with "snow" and "race."

course	board	car	horse
shoe	fall	track	storm

<u>snow</u>   <u>race</u>

snow _____ race _____

snow _____ race _____

snow _____ race _____

snow _____ race _____

Reading Lesson 7 — Student Version

C. Decoding Practice

Strategy 4: Prefixes and Suffixes

Sometimes the base word can change if we add a suffix. For example, if the base word ends in a silent "e" and the suffix begins with a vowel, you must drop the "e."
Examples: "love" + "ing" = "loving"   "fame" + "ous" = "famous"

Directions:
Cross out the silent "e" in each base word. Add the suffix to make a new word.

example:
joke + ing = **joking**

ice + ing = _____

hope + ing = _____

take + ing = _____

Directions: Choose 2 of the new words and write your own sentences using them.

_____

_____

_____

_____

Reading Lesson 7   Student Version

D. Numbers

Directions: Write the numeral next to the number.

seven		nine	
three		eight	
two		four	
six		five	
ten		one	

Reading Lesson 7

E. Sight Words

Directions: Choose the right word from the box and write it in the sentence.

up	once	down
thank	over	find

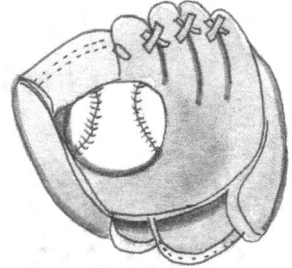

example:
1) "Be sure to **thank** grandpa for the new baseball mitt."

2) Seth sat _____ at his desk to write a card.

3) He only needed to write it _____ .

4) Mom was glad that task was _____ .

5) "Now I'll _____ my baseball and practice."

6) The ball was _____ on the shelf in his room.

F. Vocabulary

Directions: Read each new word and meaning.

plunge: to leap or dive into

legend: a story coming down from the past

oyster: a shellfish you can eat and has a rough uneven shell

urgently: calling for immediate action

transformed: changed completely

Reading Lesson 7   Student Version

G. Cloze Reading

Directions: Fill in the blank spaces with the right words from the box.

| plank | tightly | boy | cross |
| willow | grabbed | galloped | next |

The Legend of the Golden Oyster

Once upon a time there lived a **boy** named Troy. On a cold, snowy day, he was walking on a wide plank that crossed over a shallow river. Just then an ugly troll who lived below the _____ bolted to the top.

"Halt! I will not let you _____ the river until you show me the Golden Oyster. You will find it in a hole _____ to the willow tree."

Troy ran urgently to the _____ tree. He plunged down a deep hole covered by snow. In the darkness, the Golden Oyster magically glowed with a yellow light so he _____ it. Holding it _____, he ran back to the troll.

"Oh! Thank you! I am overjoyed" exclaimed the troll as he touched the oyster. Suddenly, he was transformed into a beautiful golden horse and _____ away.

Intermediate Reading

Reading Lesson 7

Student Version

H. Written Response

Directions: Read each question and answer with a complete sentence.

1) What did Troy need to cross?

2) What did Troy give to the troll?

3) What happened to the troll?

Reading Lesson 7   Student Version

I. Vowel Sound Practice

The "oy" sound. Read these "oy" words, then draw a picture for each in the empty box.

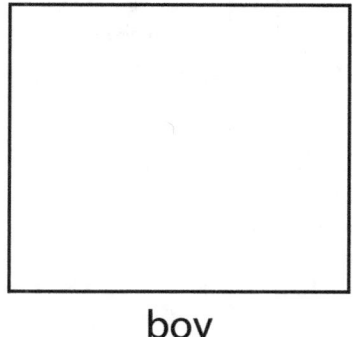 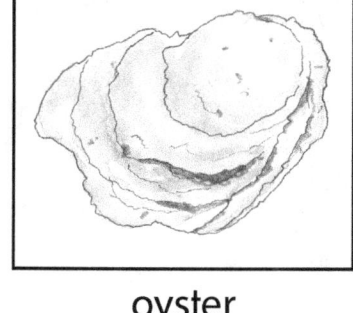 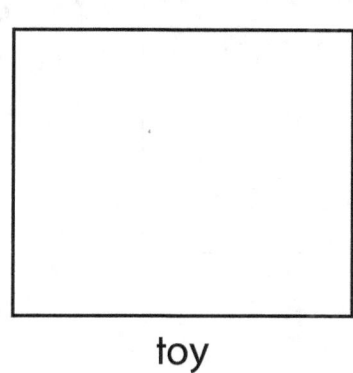

      boy   oyster   toy

The "ol" sound. Write "ol" to complete each word, then write the word in the empty space.

sc ___ d   m ___ ding

r ___ led   c ___ dest

The "ow" sound. Draw a circle around the words with the "ow" pattern.

fellow	dragon	goat	billow	game
soft	blowing	steeple	lazy	shallow

The "soft g" sound. Read these "soft g" words, then draw a picture for each.

 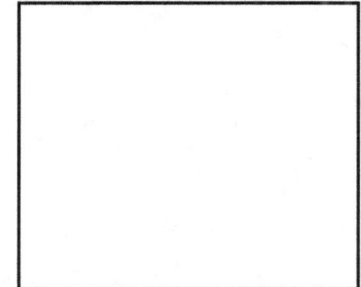

     giant   giraffe   angel

Reading Lesson 7

Student Version

J. Spelling Practice

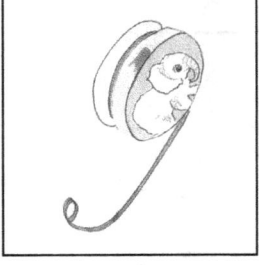

"oy" as in "toy"
Write three words with "oy" in them.

"ol" as in "oldest"
Write three words with "ol" in them.

"ow" as in "pillow"
Draw a pillow in the box. Then write three words with "ow" in them.

"g" as in "giant"
Draw a giant in the box. Then write three words with "g" in them.

Reading Lesson 7 Student Version

K. Write a Descriptive Paragraph

Directions: Students brainstorm as a group what their favorite activities are. Teacher records answers on the board and students then work independently.

One of my favorite things to do is

Directions: After you write your paragraph, draw a picture of it in this box.

Intermediate Reading

Reading Lesson 7 *Student Version*

L. Verb Tenses

Verbs are Action Words. When you look at their tense, they tell you when the action took place.

- **Present:** the action is taking place in the present moment
- **Past:** the action took place in the past
- **Future:** the action will take place in the future

Directions: Fill in the blank boxes with the correct verb.

Present	Past (add "d" or "ed")	Future (add "will")
example: bake	baked	will bake
look		
end		
squeeze		
chatter		
smash		
squirm		
nibble		
scramble		

page 88

Startup Learning

Lesson 8

Reading Lesson 8

Student Version

A. Vowel Teams

Directions: Highlight the vowel team and read each word.

"cial" and "tial" say /shul/ as in "gla<u>cial</u>"

artificial   facial   official   social
superficial   initial   essential   judicial
substantial   special   potential   partial

"<u>au</u>" says /aw/ as in "astron<u>au</u>t"

launch   autumn   pause   sauce
applaud   autograph   August   aunt
laundry   daughter   caught   taught

"<u>wa</u>" says /wä/ as in "<u>wa</u>terfall"

wash   watch   swan   walk
swat   want   waffle   wallet
swamp   wasp   wand   swallow

Reading Lesson 8   Student Version

B. Spelling Practice

Directions: First, highlight the vowel team in each word. Next, write these words in the correct vowel section.

Word List - New Vowel Teams

1. espe<u>cial</u>ly ✓
2. <u>au</u>tumn ✓
3. pre<u>wa</u>sh ✓
4. facial
5. watch
6. official
7. caught
8. swan
9. daughter
10. waffle
11. specialized

"cial" says /shul/ as in "gla<u>cial</u>"

example: espe<u>cial</u>ly

"au" says /aw/ as in "astron<u>au</u>t"

example: <u>au</u>tumn

"wa" says /wä/ as in "<u>wa</u>terfall"

example: pre<u>wa</u>sh

Intermediate Reading

Reading Lesson 8 — Student Version

C. Decoding Practice

Syllable Strategy Review:
Which syllable rule do you use to divide words into syllables?

Sort each word into the correct column.

1. hundred	5. absentee	9. remind	13. Venus
2. immense	6. helpful	10. sequel	14. puppet
3. teacher	7. never	11. teaspoon	
4. critic	8. pineapple	12. unleash	

Syllable Rules

Rule #1	Rule #2	Rule #3	Rule #4
Look for Two Consonants Together	Look for Compound Words	Look for Open or Closed Syllable	Look for a Prefix or Suffix

Rule #1 — Double Same Consonants
example: soc/cer
1. _____
2. _____

Rule #1 — Double Different Consonants
example: nap/kin
1. _____
2. _____

Rule #2 — 2 Words Make 1 Word
example: base + ball = baseball
1. pineapple
2. teaspoon

Rule #3 — Open Syllable (syllable ends with a vowel)
example: mi/nus
1. _____
2. _____

Rule #3 — Closed Syllable (the vowel is between two consonants)
example: fin/ish
1. _____
2. _____

Rule #4 — Prefixes:
example: re/heat
1. _____
2. _____

Rule #4 — Suffixes:
example: end/less
1. _____
2. _____

Reading Lesson 8   Student Version

D. Sight Words

Directions: Choose the right word from the box and write it in the sentence.

moved	this	how
many	sometimes	food

example:
1) "Instead of that, use __this__ sauce on the vegetables."

2) We get a lot of our _____ from the garden.

3) Her daughter _____ picks the carrots.

4) Mom uses _____ beans in the salad.

5) "This is _____ you make a stew."

6) We _____ the tomatoes to a new spot.

E. Vocabulary

Directions: Read each new word and meaning.

initially: in the beginning

special: set apart from the rest

cavern: a natural series of underground rooms

essential: absolutely necessary

record: write down on paper

Reading Lesson 8

F. Cloze Reading

Directions: Fill in the blank spaces with the right words from the box.

people	food	birds	flies
net	grew	Caverns	old

Cave Swallows

In 1966, three pairs of birds initially moved into Carlsbad Caverns. These special little **birds** nested inside this giant cave in New Mexico. Soon, the number of Cave Swallows grew and _____.

A scientist named Steve West catches the swallows with a _____ at one cave opening. Later, he puts numbered tags on them. Steve teaches people how to put a tiny metal band on a bird's leg. Each band has a different number. The _____ record the location, date, and size.

Sometimes a bird is caught later. Then, people can tell how _____ it is. They know how far away it _____ in the winter. They can tell if the swallow is getting the essential _____ it needs. The Cave Swallows are thriving very well at Carlsbad _____. There are more than eleven hundred!

page 94

Reading Lesson 8 — Student Version

G. Written Response

Directions: Read each question and answer with a complete sentence.

1) What birds made the caverns their home?

2) How does the scientist Steve West catch the swallows?

3) Who puts a numbered tag on the leg of each bird?

Reading Lesson 8

Student Version

H. Vowel Sound Practice

The "au" sound. Read these words with the "au" spelling. Then draw a picture for each in the empty box.

autumn   astronaut   applaud

The "cial" and "tial" sound. Write "cial" or "tial" to complete each word. Then write the whole word in the empty space.

spe _____

ini _____

par _____

so _____

The "wa" sound. Draw a circle around the words with the "wa" pattern.

| prewash | gentle | waffles | fluffy | waterfall |
| swampy | starlight | watch | kindly | gauze |

page 96   Startup Learning

Reading Lesson 8

Student Version

I. Spelling Practice

"ial" as in "glacial"
Draw a glacial scene in the box. Then write three words with "ial" in them.

"au" as in "saucer"
Draw a saucer in the box. Then write three words with "au" in them.

"wa" as in "swan"
Draw a swan in the box. Then write three words with "wa" in them.

Intermediate Reading

Reading Lesson 8

Student Version

J. Write a Persuasive Paragraph

A persuasive paragraph convinces someone to do something or change their mind. You're going to write a persuasive paragraph beginning with: "My parents should let me..." Choose a topic from the list below, and come up with 2-3 reasons to support your argument.

- play Pokemon cards
- open my own computer account
- own a bike
- have a rabbit for a pet
- stay up late at night

Use the brainstorming box to write your ideas:

Reading Lesson 8
Student Version

J. Write a Persuasive Paragraph

Directions: Begin writing your paragraph here.

_____
_____
_____
_____
_____
_____
_____
_____

Directions: After you write your paragraph, draw a picture of it in this box.

Intermediate Reading

Reading Lesson 8

Student Version

K. Contractions

Directions: Draw a line from the words on the left to their contraction.

are not	isn't
can not	mustn't
could not	don't
would not	aren't
is not	didn'tv
do not	can't
does not	wouldn't
did not	doesn't
must not	couldn't

Directions: Fill in the blank with the contraction.

example: he is — he's

example: they are — they're

he would _____
she would _____

here is _____
she is _____

I would _____
there is _____

I will _____
you will _____

I am _____
they will _____

it is _____
we are _____

Reading Lesson 9

A. Vowel Teams

Directions: Highlight the vowel team and read each word.

"ie" says /ee/ as in "berries"

cookie   piece   beanie   prairie
goalie   relief   carries   copier
believe   studied tidied   briefcase

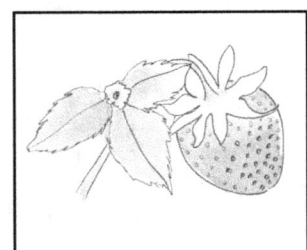

"tur" says /chur/ as in "creature"

nature   furniture   capture   future
texture adventure   pasture   gesture
lecture feature   fracture posture

soft "g" says /j/ when an "e" "i" or "y" follows it as in "giraffe"

cage   danger   strange   stage
ginger   page   gentle   gym
vegetable magic   largest   giant

Reading Lesson 9
Student Version

B. Spelling Practice

Directions: First, highlight the vowel team in each word. Next, write these words in the correct vowel section.

Word List - New Vowel Teams

1. ach**ie**ve ✓
2. adven**tur**ing ✓
3. a**g**e ✓
4. believing
5. capture
6. cookies
7. furniture
8. ginger
9. ecology
10. goalie
11. nature

"g" says /j/ before e, i or y

example: a**g**e

"tur" says /chr/ as in "creature"

example: adven**tur**ing

"ie" says /ee/ as in "berries"

example: ach**ie**ve

Intermediate Reading

Reading Lesson 9

Student Version

C. Decoding Practice

Syllable Strategy Review:
Which syllable rule do you use to divide words into syllables?

Sort each word into the correct column.

1. suppose	5. redo	9. skateboard	13. veto
2. pamphlet	6. canine	10. thicker	14. weekend
3. channel	7. dislike	11. trumpet	
4. volume	8. weekly	12. vanish	

Syllable Rules

Rule #1	Rule #2	Rule #3	Rule #4
Look for Two Consonants Together	Look for Compound Words	Look for Open or Closed Syllable	Look for a Prefix or Suffix
Double Same Consonants example: soc/cer 1. _____ 2. _____	**2 Words Make 1 Word** example: base + ball = baseball 1. skateboard _____ _____ 2. weekend _____	**Open Syllable** (syllable ends with a vowel) example: mi/nus 1. _____ 2. _____	**Prefixes:** example: re/heat 1. _____ 2. _____
Double Different Consonants example: nap/kin 1. _____ 2. _____		**Closed Syllable** (the vowel is between two consonants) example: fin/ish 1. _____ 2. _____	**Suffixes:** example: end/less 1. _____ 2. _____

Reading Lesson 9　　　　　　　　　　Student Version

D. Sight Words

Directions: Choose the right word from the box and write it in the sentence.

again	everyone	should
toward		there

example:
1) Why don't you ring the bell **again** ?

2) That way, _____ can hear it.

3) All the children _____ come inside now.

4) The children over _____ need to be told.

5) Have them move _____ the front of the line.

E. Vocabulary

Directions: Read each new word and meaning.

capture: to catch and take hold of something or someone from another team in a game or war

retrieve: to take back something

stubborn: when someone is not willing to accept help or listen when someone else tells them what to do

Reading Lesson 9 Student Version

F. Cloze Reading

Directions: Fill in the blank spaces with the right words from the box.

team	flag	point	orange
zone	Anna	children	blue

Capture the Flag

On a warm day in May, the energetic children played "Capture the Flag." Ms. Priestly, the gym teacher, divided them into two teams on the field. She hung one _____ and one _____ flag on the fences at either end. Anna's team went first. She ran around the other team to the fence where no one could tag her. She was relieved to be in the safe _____ .

"Anna! Retrieve that orange flag!" yelled her teammate Ling. "Now pass it to me." But _____ was stubborn and believed she could return to the center line with the flag. However, she only ran briefly before Keyon from the other _____ grabbed the _____ and ran over the middle line. He felt so great to capture the flag and achieve the first _____ of the game.

Reading Lesson 9   Student Version

G. Written Response

Directions: Read each question and answer with a complete sentence.

1) How many teams does "Capture the Flag" need?

2) Why didn't Anna pass the orange flag to Ling?

3) Who captured the flag to win the first point of the game?

Reading Lesson 9

Student Version

H. Vowel Sound Practice

The "ie" sound. Read these words with the "ie" spelling. Then draw a picture for each in the empty box.

cookie   berries   briefcase

The "tur" sound. Write "tur" to complete each word. Then write the whole word in the empty space.

na _____ e _____

crea _____ e _____

pas _____ e _____

fu _____ e _____

The soft "g" sound. Draw a circle around the words with the soft "g" pattern.

| page | funny | gentle | ginger | time |
| honey | magic | playful | different | gloves |

Reading Lesson 9

Student Version

I. Spelling Practice

"ie" as in "cookie"
Draw a cookie in the box. Then write three words with "ie" in them.

"tur" as in "nature"
Draw a scene from nature in the box. Then write three words with "tur" in them.

"g" as in "vegetable"
Draw a vegetable in the box. Then write three words with soft "g" in them.

Intermediate Reading

Reading Lesson 9   Student Version

J. Word Choice

What do you think Word Choice means in writing? Circle all words that apply:

- grammar
- interesting nouns
- vivid verbs
- punctuation
- exciting adjectives
- presentation
- ideas

Words can help paint a picture for your reader. Words are vitally important tools for a writer.

Can you write down some silly words that come to mind? Like gooey, hunky dory, baloney, loony, slimy …

_____

_____

Can you write some vivid verbs like shuffle, glide, cling, amble, burrow, stroll?

_____

_____

Excellent word choice is like sprinkles on ice cream:
- Like sprinkles on ice cream
- Like salt on eggs
- Like the diamond on a ring

page 110   Startup Learning

Reading Lesson 9

Student Version

J. Word Choice

Can you find some words that sound in real life just the way they are written like moo, meow, boom?

Can you fill in the list below with descriptive, sensory words?

Taste:

Touch:

Smell:

Sight:

Sound:

| Reading Lesson 9 | | Student Version |

K. Fun With Idioms

Idioms are phrases that have a common meaning that is not the literal one.

<u>Directions</u>: Draw a picture of what each idiom seems to mean and then write what it *really* means.

Idiom	What is seems to mean	What it really means
cat nap		
hit the books		
easy as pie		

<u>Super Challenge</u>: Write a sentence using your favorite idiom.

Reading Lesson 9 — Student Version

L. Descriptive Words

Use **adjectives**, describing words, to add fascinating details to your writing and make your ideas more precise.

Directions: Highlight or underline your 2 favorite adjectives from the list below:

Overused Word	Use one of these instead
bad	awful, disgusting, terrible, unpleasant
big	enormous, gigantic, immense, towering
fun	amusing, enjoyable, entertaining, exciting
good	fantastic, incredible, magnificent, wonderful
got	acquired, collected, obtained, received
great	astounding, marvelous, splendid, terrific
nice	charming, friendly, pleasant, warmhearted
pretty	attractive, beautiful, gorgeous, handsome, lovely

Directions: Circle the adjectives in the following sentences, and underline the noun they describe.

example:
Sarah has an (adorable) (fluffy) (brown) puppet.

I watched the shiny, big jet fly away.

Samir wrapped himself in a thick, wool blanket.

Please take out all those messy, oily rags.

Please erase those stray, black marks.

Let's go to the pretty, new store on Main Street.

Where is my old, red hat?

Lesson 10

Reading Lesson 10

A. Vowel Teams

Directions: Highlight the vowel team and read each word.

"ear" says /ār/ as in "bear"

tear   unbearable   bearcat   swearing
pear   teardown   neckwear   bearskin
wear   outerwear   swear   wearing

"dg" says /j/ as in "bridge"

edge   ledge   hedge   pledge
ridge   badge   fudge   judge
nudge   smudge   dodge   wedge

soft "oo" says /ü/ as in "books"

hook   hood   took   shook
cook   mistook   roof   good
nook   crooked   goodbye   looked

"ea" says /ē/ as in "leaves"

peach   beak   stream   eat
beach   reach   cream   mealtime
teacher   seaside   read   seatbelts

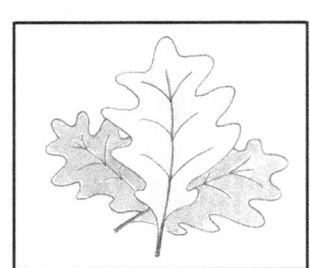

Reading Lesson 10   Student Version

B. Spelling Practice

Directions: First, highlight the vowel team in each word. Next, write these words in the correct vowel section.

Word List - New Vowel Teams

1. wearing ✓
2. pledge ✓
3. shook ✓
4. dream
5. fudge
6. childhood
7. tearing
8. seaside
9. prejudge
10. bearable
11. mistook

"ear" says /ār/ as in "bear"

example: wearing

"dg" says /j/ as in "bridge"

example: pledge

"oo" says /ü/ as in "book"

example: shook

"ea" says /ē/ as in "leaves"

example: dream

Reading Lesson 10 — Student Version

C. Decoding Practice

Syllable Strategy Review:
Which syllable rule do you use to divide words into syllables?

Sort each word into the correct column.

1. traffic	5. driven	9. tearing	13. mimic
2. survive	6. preheat	10. drawbridge	14. prevent
3. beanstalk	7. wearing	11. fantastic	
4. collector	8. hero	12. robot	

Syllable Rules

Rule #1	Rule #2	Rule #3	Rule #4
Look for Two Consonants Together	Look for Compound Words	Look for Open or Closed Syllable	Look for a Prefix or Suffix
Double Same Consonants example: soc/cer 1. _____ 2. _____	**2 Words Make 1 Word** example: base + ball = baseball 1. drawbridge 2. beanstalk	**Open Syllable** (syllable ends with a vowel) example: mi/nus 1. _____ 2. _____	**Prefixes:** example: re/heat 1. _____ 2. _____
Double Different Consonants example: nap/kin 1. _____ 2. _____		**Closed Syllable** (the vowel is between two consonants) example: fin/ish 1. _____ 2. _____	**Suffixes:** example: end/less 1. _____ 2. _____

Reading Lesson 10   Student Version

D. Sight Words

Directions: Choose the right word from the box and write it in the sentence.

| beautiful | neighborhood | were |
| they | | to |

example:
1) There is a beekeeper in our **neighborhood**.

2) She invited us to see the _____ beehive.

3) We went _____ her house on Monday.

4) The bees _____ very active.

5) _____ made lots of buzzing noise.

E. Vocabulary

Directions: Read each new word and meaning.

collected: brought together

leaned: move into a sloping position

pretend: make something appear to be something else.

Reading Lesson 10

F. Cloze Reading

CCSS.ELA-LITERACY.RF.2.4

Directions: Fill in the blank spaces with the right words from the box.

skipped	slow	surface	pretend
side	real	stick	wade

Skipping Stones

On a beautiful day, the children decided to play in the park. "Wear your old shoes so we can **wade** in the stream," reminded Keyon.

At the park, they collected wood sticks and leaves for races. At the top of the old bridge, they dropped a leaf and a _____ into the _____ moving stream on one _____.

Then they ran to the other side to look for the one that came out first. Next, Kurt pretended to cook hamburgers over a _____ grill. Then they ate the _____ pears and fudge that Anna brought. After that, they looked for small, flat stones and skipped them along the _____ of the water. Anna's _____ three times and Kurt's skipped five times. Ling leaned way back before she let her stone skim the water. It skipped eight times!

Reading Lesson 10

Student Version

G. Written Response

Directions: Read each question and answer with a complete sentence.

1) Where did the children play?

2) What did the kids pretend to have?

3) Whose stone skipped on the water eight times?

Reading Lesson 10

Student Version

H. Vowel Sound Practice

The "ear" sound. Read these "ear" words, then draw a picture for each in the empty box.

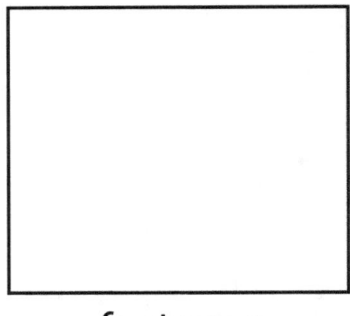
footwear

bear

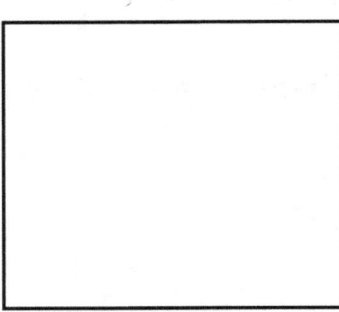
swimwear

The "dg" sound. Write "dg" to complete each word, then write the word in the empty space.

ju___ed   ri___e

ba___e   lo___e

The "oo" sound. Draw a circle around the words with the "oo" pattern.

| woolen | caterpillar | patio | chairs | hood |
| barbeque | cement | cooking | charcoal | mistook |

The "ea" sound. Read these "ea" words, then draw a picture for each.

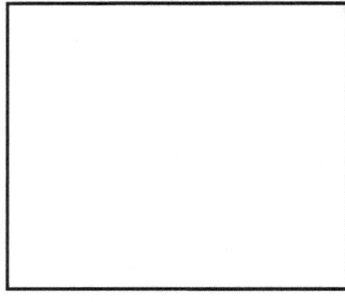
stream

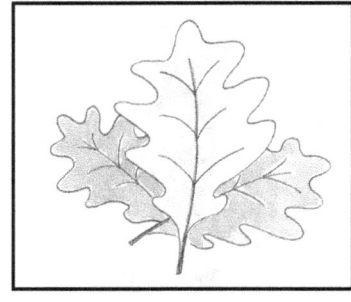
leaves

peach

Reading Lesson 10

Student Version

I. Spelling Practice

"ear" as in "bear"
Draw a bear in the box. Then write three words with "ear" in them.

"dg" as in "bridge"
Draw a bridge in the box. Then write three words with "dg" in them.

"oo" as in "roof"
Draw a roof in the box. Then write three words with "oo" in them.

"ea" as in "sea"
Draw a sea in the box. Then write three words with "ea" in them.

Intermediate Reading

Reading Lesson 10

Student Version

J. Write an Imaginative Paragraph

The teacher will provide many pictures from magazines to use as prompts for your next writing assignment. Select one. Use your imagination and write a story based on the picture and tape or paste the photo in your paper.

Example:

Let me tell you, this is the best place to swim to for eating well. Our little pod has just traveled up here from California and my, oh my! The food is so tasty even though I swallow most of it whole. Who needs to chew? In fact, I swallow salmon and flounder in as few bites as possible, too. These fish are hard to outswim and grab but maybe that's why they're so satisfying! Now, the ocean water here is especially cold so it takes a lot of energy to keep warm and of course, all those fish give us lots of energy. Despite the chilly temperature, we keep coming back here for the delicious, plentiful fish.

Directions: Now, write your rough draft of your Imaginative Narrative Paragraph on the next page. Have fun with this paper and let your Sparkling Voice shine through!

Reading Lesson 10

Student Version

J. Write an Imaginative Paragraph

Rough draft:

_____

_____

_____

_____

_____

_____

_____

_____

_____

Let's look at how you can revise your paper. After revising by yourself, exchange with a classmate and have them give you suggestions.

- Did you begin many sentences with "I"? Revise most of those!
- Did you write any short sentences? Make them longer! Combine sentences.
- Did you use any vivid verbs? If not, write some now!
- Did you choose good words to describe things?
- Did you use transitions?

Reading Lesson 10

J. Write an Imaginative Paragraph

Final draft:

Lesson 11

STARTUP LEARNING

Reading Lesson 11

Student Version

A. Vowel Teams

Directions: Highlight the vowel team and read each word.

"ea" says /ĕ/ as in "bread"

head   spread   already   feather
heavy   breakfast thread   ahead
weather heaven   treasure   instead

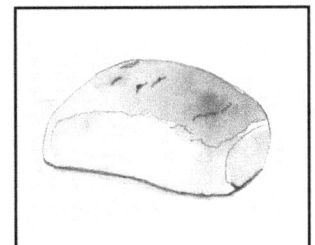

"ey" says /ē/ as in "monkey"

valley   donkey   turkey   honey
chimney   money   trolley   hockey
volleyball journey barley   flakey

"sch" says /sk/ as in "school"

schooner   scholar
schedule   scheme

"ear" says /r/ as in "earth"

search early   learn   earthquake
yearn   earnings   heard   rehearse
earn   relearned   pearl   searching

Reading Lesson 11 — Student Version

B. Spelling Practice

Directions: First, highlight the vowel team in each word. Next, write these words in the correct vowel section.

Word List - New Vowel Teams

1. spr<u>ea</u>d ✓
2. hock<u>ey</u> ✓
3. <u>sch</u>edule ✓
4. h<u>ear</u>d
5. keyboard
6. scholar
7. heavy
8. learning
9. feather
10. rehearse
11. kidney

"<u>ea</u>" says /ĕ/ as in "br<u>ea</u>d"

example: spr<u>ea</u>d

"<u>ey</u>" says /ē/ as in "k<u>ey</u>"

example: monk<u>ey</u>

"<u>sch</u>" says /sk/ as in "<u>sch</u>ool"

example: <u>sch</u>edule

"<u>ear</u>" says /r/ as in "<u>ear</u>th"

example: h<u>ear</u>d

Reading Lesson 11

Student Version

C. Decoding Practice

Syllable Strategy Review:
Which syllable rule do you use to divide words into syllables?

Sort each word into the correct column.

1. survey	5. learning	9. trolley	13. limit
2. schoolhouse	6. earthquake	10. research	14. pretzel
3. native	7. moment	11. travel	
4. dismiss	8. speaker	12. written	

Syllable Rules

Rule #1	Rule #2	Rule #3	Rule #4
Look for Two Consonants Together	Look for Compound Words	Look for Open or Closed Syllable	Look for a Prefix or Suffix
Double Same Consonants example: soc/cer 1. _____ 2. _____	**2 Words Make 1 Word** example: base + ball = baseball 1. schoolhouse _____ _____	**Open Syllable** (syllable ends with a vowel) example: mi/nus 1. _____ 2. _____	**Prefixes:** example: re/heat 1. _____ 2. _____
Double Different Consonants example: nap/kin 1. _____ 2. _____	2. earthquake _____	**Closed Syllable** (the vowel is between two consonants) example: fin/ish 1. _____ 2. _____	**Suffixes:** example: end/less 1. _____ 2. _____

Reading Lesson 11   Student Version

D. Sight Words

Directions: Choose the right word from the box and write it in the sentence.

said	pull	their
were	dough	

example:
1) "Let's serve ice cream cones to our guests," **said** Mom.

2) "Everyone loves cookie _____ flavor," said Jamal.

3) "We _____ going to have rocky road," said Mom.

4) "We can let them choose _____ own flavor," said Jamal.

5) "_____ the box of cones out of the cupboard," said Mom.

E. Vocabulary

Directions: Read each new word and meaning.

schedule: list of events and times

measure: use a device to get the right amount

network: like a web that joins together

knead: work to massage or mold with the hands

Intermediate Reading   page 131

F. Passage: Baking Bread

Baking Bread

It was early in the day at school when Ms. Leathers said "Today we are going to learn how to make bread."

The students were so happy this was on their schedule. First, Ms. Leathers measured the yeast, salt, flour, honey and butter into separate bowls. Then she asked Ling to pour very warm water in the bowl with the yeast and stir it.

"Yeast is a living plant that grows in warm, moist dough. It gives off bubbles of gas. These bubbles cause the dough to rise," said Ms. Leathers.

After Keyon stirred in the honey and salt, Ms. Leathers added

"The honey will help the yeast produce gas bubbles, too."

Kurt emptied the flour and melted butter into the bowl.

"The butter will make our bread tender. The flour contains a protein called gluten. The gluten stretches to form a network around the gas bubbles," explained Ms. Leathers.

She made a ball with the dough and began to knead it on the counter top. To knead the dough, she pushed and pulled and punched it with the heels of her hands. Then all the students took turns to push and pull and punch the dough. Everyone felt great pleasure from kneading the bread dough. Afterwards, Ms. Leathers put the ball of dough in a bowl in a warm oven to let it rise. The smell of the yeast made Kurt yearn to eat it. Instead, they all had to wait for several hours. Finally, it was shaped and baked. They treasured each slice of buttered, delicious, healthy bread.

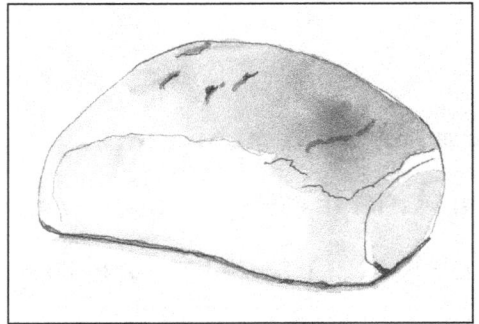

Reading Lesson 11

Student Version

G. Written Response

Directions: Read each question and answer with a complete sentence.

1) What is yeast? (list at least 2 things)

2) What is the protein in the flour called?

3) What will help the yeast produce gas bubbles?

Reading Lesson 11

Student Version

H. Vowel Sound Practice

The "ea" sound. Read these "ea" words, then draw a picture for each in the empty box.

breakfast

feather

thread

The "ey" sound. Write "ey" to complete each word, then write the word in the empty space.

voll_____   hon_____

turk_____   barl_____

The "sch" sound. Draw a circle around the words with the "sch" pattern.

| flexible | scholar | lightning | swimming | schooner |
| schedule | shining | school | shaking | scurry |

The "ear" sound. Read these "ear" words, then draw a picture for each.

searchlight

Earth

pearl

Reading Lesson 11

Student Version

I. Spelling Practice

"ea" as in "bread"
Draw bread in the box. Then write three words with "ea" in them.

"ey" as in "monkey"
Draw a monkey in the box. Then write three words with "ey" in them.

"sch" as in "school"
Draw a school in the box. Then write three words with "sch" in them.

"ear" as in "Earth"
Draw the Earth in the box. Then write three words with "ea" in them.

Reading Lesson 11

J. Write a Personal Narrative

Directions: First, select a topic from the following list. This will be a true story, so think of an example from your own life that matches the topic you choose:

- The funniest thing I ever saw
- The person I admire the most
- My most embarrassing moment
- The time I got lost
- The most wonderful gift I've ever received

Example:

Learning to Swim

Learning something new can be a scary experience. One of the hardest things I've ever had to do was learn to swim. First, I walked out of the locker room with my swimsuit on and stood by the pool, nervous for everyone to show up. After a few minutes, the teacher arrived. She smiled, introduced herself, and two more students joined us. I started to feel more relaxed. Next, the teacher gave us water wings to help us float and kickboards to help us practice kicking.

Sooner than I imagined, the kicking and arm movements began to feel "right" and I was able to swim! It was a wonderful feeling - like soaring! Learning to swim was not easy for me, but in the end my hard work was worth it.

Reading Lesson 11 Student Version

J. Write a Personal Narrative

Now, write an outline for your narrative:

Topic sentence:

Detail 1:

Detail 2:

Detail 3:

Concluding sentence:

Reading Lesson 11

Student Version

J. Write a Personal Narrative

Write your rough draft:

Reading Lesson 11

Student Version

J. Write a Personal Narrative

Write your final draft:

Lesson 12

Reading Lesson 12

A. Vowel Teams

Directions: Highlight the vowel team and read each word.

"aw" says /ô/ as in "str<u>aw</u>berry"

awe	claw	saw	draw
thaw	paw	raw	straw
coleslaw	crawl	dawn	hawk

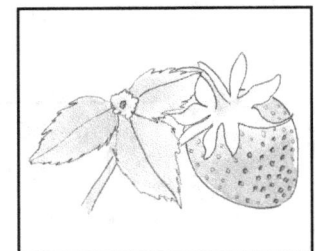

"ough" says /ō/ as in "d<u>ough</u>nut"

although   thorough

sourdough

schwa "o" says /ə/ as in "m<u>o</u>ney"

come	from	some	done
month	become	brother	mother
bottom	nothing	among	common

"ei" says /ā/ as in "l<u>ei</u>"

eight	vein	weigh	neighbor
dreidl	reigns	sleigh	reindeer
veil	skein	unveil	paperweight

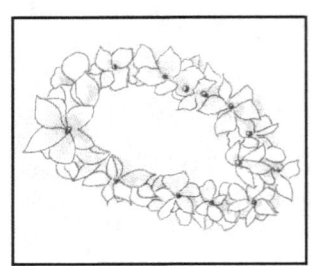

Reading Lesson 12 — Student Version

B. Spelling Practice

Directions: First, highlight the vowel team in each word. Next, write these words in the correct vowel section.

Word List - New Vowel Teams

1. gn<u>aw</u> ✓
2. th<u>orough</u> ✓
3. br<u>o</u>ther ✓
4. b<u>ei</u>ge ✓
5. sourdough
6. bottom
7. redraw
8. veil
9. yawning
10. Monday
11. although

"aw" says /ô/ as in "str<u>aw</u>berry"

example: gn<u>aw</u>

"ough" says /ō/ as in "d<u>ough</u>nut"

example: th<u>orough</u>

schwa "o" says /ə/ as in "m<u>o</u>ney"

example: br<u>o</u>ther

"ei" says /ā/ as in "l<u>ei</u>"

example: b<u>ei</u>ge

Reading Lesson 12

Student Version

C. Decoding Practice

Syllable Strategy Review:
Which syllable rule do you use to divide words into syllables?

Sort each word into the correct column.

1. gallon	5. yawning	9. unveil	13. rocket
2. jawbone	6. tropic	10. rubbish	14. longest
3. zero	7. doughnut	11. termite	
4. redraw	8. inquire	12. bonus	

Syllable Rules

Rule #1	Rule #2	Rule #3	Rule #4
Look for Two Consonants Together	Look for Compound Words	Look for Open or Closed Syllable	Look for a Prefix or Suffix
Double Same Consonants example: soc/cer 1. _____ 2. _____	**2 Words Make 1 Word** example: base + ball = baseball 1. doughnut _____ _____ 2. jawbone _____ _____	**Open Syllable** (syllable ends with a vowel) example: mi/nus 1. _____ 2. _____	**Prefixes:** example: re/heat 1. _____ 2. _____
Double Different Consonants example: nap/kin 1. _____ 2. _____		**Closed Syllable** (the vowel is between two consonants) example: fin/ish 1. _____ 2. _____	**Suffixes:** example: end/less 1. _____ 2. _____

Reading Lesson 12   Student Version

D. Sight Words

Directions: Choose the right word from the box and write it in the sentence.

friend	neighbors	from
	was	come

example:
1) Maybe our **neighbors** will be at the Chinese New Year Parade.

2) My _____ Ling will be there.

3) Does the parade come _____ the park?

4) Can Paul and Anya _____ , too?

5) I was going to go last year but I _____ traveling.

E. Vocabulary

Directions: Read each new word and meaning.

focus: the center of interest or activity

covered: put something on top of

weighted: hold something down

drawing: a picture made with a pen or pencil or crayon

Intermediate Reading   page 145

Reading Lesson 12

F. Cloze Reading

<u>Directions</u>: **Fill in the blank spaces with the right words from the box.**

| lonely | imagination | side | garden |
| top | red | help | there |

Drawing Lesson

Today Anna's mother, Mrs. Lough, came to her class to give a drawing lesson.

She led eight students to the **garden** to sit on straw covered paths.

"Find one plant or animal to draw. Then work quietly," taught Anna's mother.

"Will you _____ me draw these strawberries?" asked Keyon.

"Yes, you ought to shade this _____,

the one away from the light," suggested Mrs. Lough.

Once Ling saw a _____-tailed hawk, she began to draw it.

The big hawk landed on _____ of the tree! After erasing a flaw

in her picture, Anna continued to draw a caterpillar.

"Ling, you have brought your _____ to this work!" laughed Mrs.

Lough. For when she saw Ling's drawing, _____ were two hawks.

"It looked _____ so I added a friend for him," she replied.

Reading Lesson 12 **Student Version**

G. Written Response

Directions: Read each question and answer with a complete sentence.

1) Where does the story take place?

2) Who are the characters in the story? Name at least three.

3) Name three things the children drew.

Reading Lesson 12

Student Version

H. Vowel Sound Practice

The "aw" sound. Read these "aw" words, then draw a picture for each in the empty box.

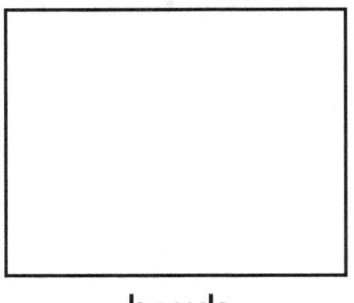
hawk

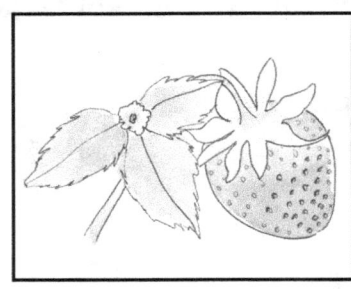
strawberry

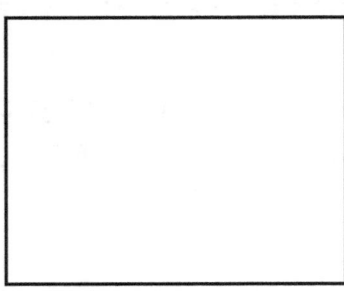
claw

The "ough" sound. Write "ough" to complete each word, then write the whole word.

thor _____

sourd _____

alth _____

The "ei" sound. Draw a circle around the words with the "ei" pattern.

| pencils | sharpener | neighbor | handy | sleigh |
| candles | stores | reign | weigh | unveil |

The schwa "o" sound. Read these "o" words, then draw a picture for each.

mother

money

brother

Reading Lesson 12

Student Version

I. Spelling Practice

"aw" as in "paw"

Draw a paw in the box. Then write three words with "aw" in them.

"ough" as in "doughnut"

Draw a doughnut in the box. Then write three words with "ough" in them.

"o" as in "oven"

Draw an oven in the box. Then write three words with the schwa "o" in them.

"ei" as in "reindeer"

Draw the reindeer in the box. Then write three words with "ei" in them.

Reading Lesson 12

Student Version

J. Write a Comparative Paragraph

As you have learned, organizing your thoughts before writing not only saves time, but makes your writing stronger. Strength comes from well thought out ideas. In addition, strength comes from effectively pulling your reader through your paper in a logical, orderly way.

The internal structure in a Comparative Paragraph is best organized by using a Venn Diagram. This tool allows you to visually see what ways two items are similar, different, or the same.

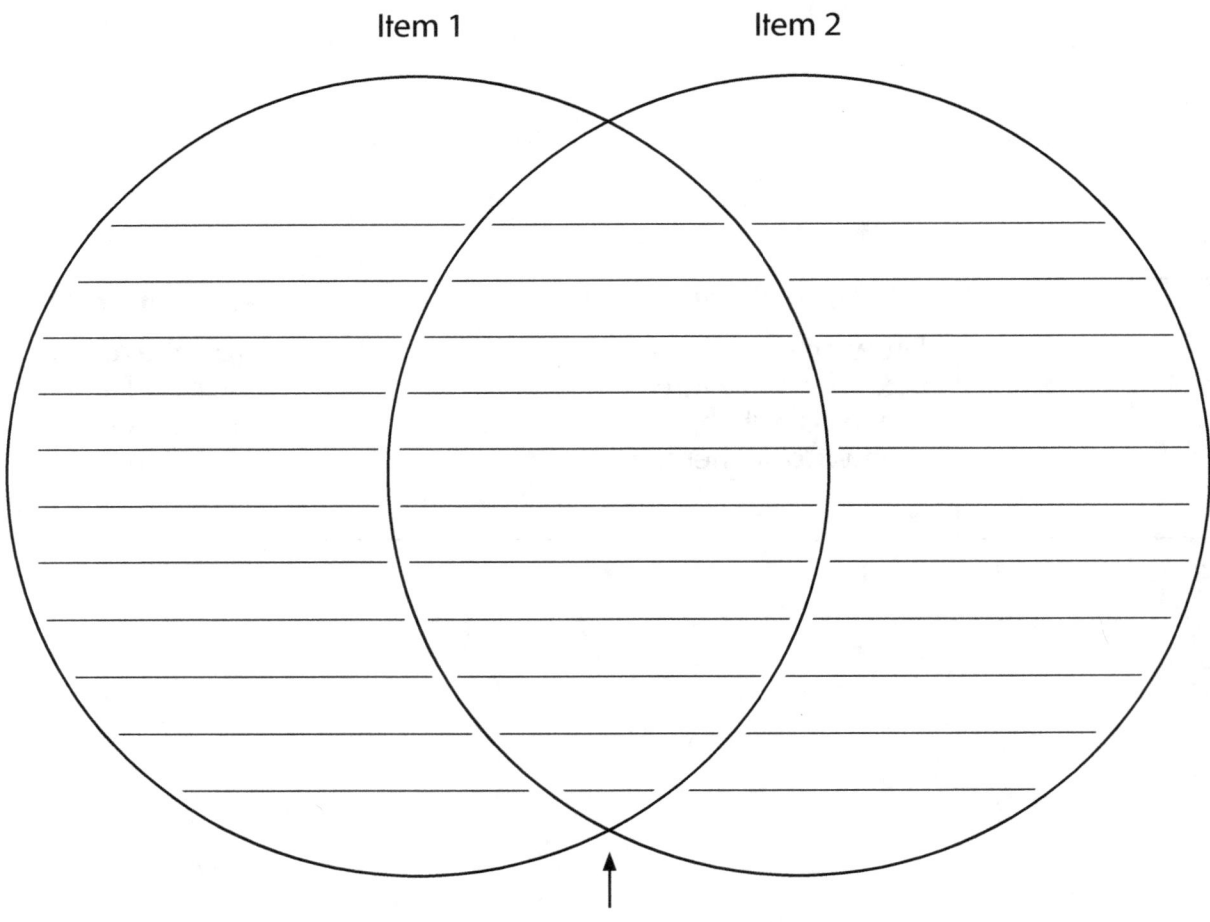

Ways that Item 1 and Item 2 are the same

Reading Lesson 12 — Student Version

J. Write a Comparative Paragraph

Directions: Compare and contrast penguins and puffins. This assignment is an example of non-fiction writing (based on facts) and expository writing (provides information). Fill in the Venn Diagram on the next page with this information.

Notes on Penguins	Notes on Puffins
sea birds	sea birds
native to southern hemisphere	native to northern hemisphere
cannot fly	can fly
black feathers, white feathers	black and white or all black feathers
raise their young on land	raise their young on land

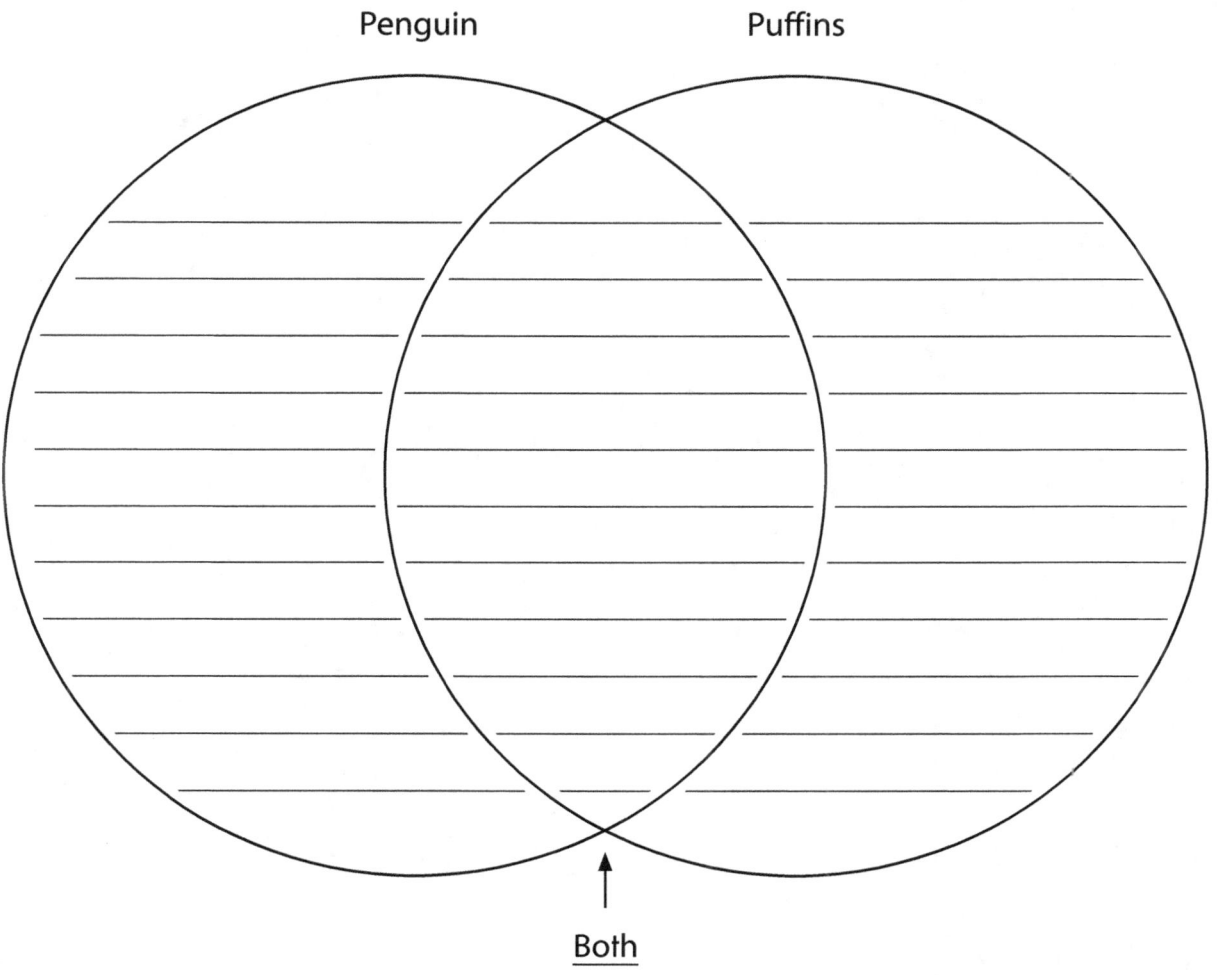

Both

Intermediate Reading

Reading Lesson 12

J. Write a Comparative Paragraph

Write your final draft:

Lesson 13

STARTUP
LEARNING

Reading Lesson 13

A. Vowel Teams

Directions: Highlight the vowel team and read each word.

"ou" says /ăō/ as in "mouse"

ouch	out	loudly	cloud
house	counted	found	surround
outline	proud	scour	ourselves

"ow" says /ăō/ as in "flower"

vowel	down	cow	town
brown	sow	towel	clown
shower	rowdy	chowder	plowing

schwa "a" says /ŭ/ as in "panda"

comma	stamina	gorilla	replica
America	formula	veranda	salsa
adorable	Montana	parka	camera

Reading Lesson 13

Student Version

B. Spelling Practice

Directions: First, highlight the vowel team in each word. Next, write these words in the correct vowel section.

Word List - New Vowel Teams

1. pound ✓
2. shower ✓
3. zebra ✓
4. downhill
5. sounded
6. eyebrow
7. Africa
8. round
9. tuna

"ou" says /ăō/ as in "mouse"

example: pound

"ow" says /ăō/ as in "flower"

example: shower

schwa "a" says /ŭ/ as in "panda"

example: zebra

Intermediate Reading

Reading Lesson 13

Student Version

C. Decoding Practice

**There are four strategies that help us divide words into syllables.
Every syllable must have a vowel.**

Strategy 1:
Dividing Words Into Syllables - Double-same/double-different consonants

Find the two middle consonants and mark a "syllable wall" inside them.
Make sure there is a vowel on either side of the syllable wall.

Example 1 - Double-same	**Example 2 - Double-different**
su f|f ix	a d|m i t
comma	expense
hiccup	chowder
muffin	umpire

Strategy 2:
Dividing Words Into Syllables - Open/closed syllables

When two consonants are not in the middle of a word, do the following:

1) Find the first vowel and put a syllable wall after it. The vowel will say its name. **This is an example of an open syllable.**

2) Make a CVC pattern (Consonant-Vowel-Consonant) and put a syllable wall after it. The vowel will make a short vowel sound. **This is an example of a closed syllable.** (the CVC pattern is highlighted in the example)

Example 1 - Open Syllables	**Example 2 - Closed Syllables**
si|lent	c v c lem|on
minus	radish
hero	level
siren	credit

Reading Lesson 13

Student Version

C. Decoding Practice

Strategy 3: Compound Words

Formed when two small words are put together to make one new big word.

Directions: Draw a line between these words to make compound words.

tooth	board
your	room
bed	paste
key	self

Directions: Circle the two words that make up each compound word.

1. c a m p f i r e
2. r a i n b o w
3. d i s h w a s h e r
4. s u n f l o w e r

Directions: Use the words in the box to form compound words with "where" and "up."

| stream | some | any | every |
| hill | load | no | date |

<u>where</u>   <u>up</u>

_____ where   up _____

_____ where   up _____

_____ where   up _____

_____ where   up _____

Reading Lesson 13

Student Version

C. Decoding Practice

Strategy 4: Prefixes and Suffixes

When adding an "s" to words that end in a consonant followed by "y," cross out the "y" and add "ies." **Example: "fly" + "s" = "flies"**

Directions: Cross out the "y" after a consonant. Then add "ies."

example:
cry + s = **cries**

dry + s =

baby + s =

try + s =

multiply + s =

Directions: Select words to complete the sentences. Add "ly" to each adverb.

| quick | slow | loud | quiet |

1) Her niece is a slow eater. She eats **slowly** .

2) Michael is a quick speller. He spells _____ .

3) Julia has a loud voice. She speaks _____ .

4) My brother is quiet when he studies. He works _____ .

Reading Lesson 13 — Student Version

D. Sight Words

Directions: Choose the right word from the box and write it in the sentence.

did	with	never
grows	found	

example:
1) I'm surprised how the air **grows** colder here.

2) _____ you bring your sweater?

3) No, but I did bring my fall coat _____ me.

4) You _____ know when the wind will get stronger.

5) I've _____ it is warmer away from the lake.

E. Vocabulary

Directions: Read each new word and meaning.

chores: regular, routine work or tasks

cousins: children of an uncle and aunt

raise: tend to the long term care of children, animals or crops

showers: rain storms

farming: the occupation of raising animals or crops

Reading Lesson 13

F. Passage: A Visit to the Farm

CCSS.ELA-LITERACY.RF.2.4

Directions: Read the story and circle the vowel teams from the list.

"<u>ou</u>" as in "m<u>ou</u>se"   "<u>ow</u>" as in "fl<u>ow</u>er"   lazy "<u>a</u>" as in "pand<u>a</u>"

My uncle and aunt have a farm in Montana. They are proud of their farm. They raise sheep, goats and chickens. While I was there last week, I did chores with my cousins. We counted the brown eggs we collected from the hen house. The roosters were rowdy crowing so loudly! When we brought the chickens food, we found ourselves surrounded by them. Later, we scoured the floor in the hen house to make it really clean.

Next, we fed the sow, the adorable mother pig. Although there were dark clouds in the sky, it never showered. So, my uncle finished plowing his fields. He turned the dirt over with his big tractor to get it ready to grow wheat, hay and barley seeds. Now I know how hard my cousins work. Farming takes a lot of stamina.

Super Challenge: Can you find the four tricky words where "ou" doesn't sound like "m<u>ou</u>se?"

Reading Lesson 13

Student Version

G. Written Response

Directions: Read each question and answer with a complete sentence.

1) Where do the cousins live?

2) What do they raise on the farm?

3) What was one chore the children did?

4) What did the uncle do?

Reading Lesson 13

Student Version

H. Vowel Sound Practice

The "ou" sound. Read these "ou" words, then draw a picture for each in the empty box.

  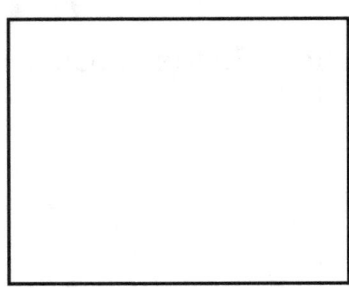

cloud   mouse   house

The "ow" sound. Write "ow" to complete each word, then write the whole word.

ch ___ der

t ___ els

d ___ nt   n ___

v ___ el

Schwa "a" sound. Draw a circle around the words with the "a" pattern.

| parka | beauty | camera | hinting | comma |
| stove | salsa | television | gorilla | dishwasher |

Reading Lesson 13

Student Version

I. Spelling Practice

"ou" as in "house"
Draw a house in the box. Then write three words with "ou" in them.

"ow" as in "cow"
Draw a cow in the box. Then write three words with "ow" in them.

"a" as in "panda"
Draw an panda in the box. Then write three words with "a" in them.

Intermediate Reading

Reading Lesson 13

Student Version

J. Ten Minute Writing

Directions: Write a descriptive paragraph answering "What is or was your favorite childhood toy?" similar to the student example below.

> **Student example:**
>
> My favorite childhood toy is my adorable stuffed mouse. I truly like her because my mom gave her to me when I turned one. She is pink and has beans in her legs. In addition, my mouse has a super pointy nose and large blue eyes. I wonder how long I'll keep her, but it'll be at least until I'm 21. Whenever I have free time at home, I play with my stuffed mouse because only she knows how to calm me down. Wait until you hold her and you'll fall in love with her. Clearly, my stuffed mouse is my most favorite toy from my childhood.

Reading Lesson 13

Student Version

J. Ten Minute Writing

Write your descriptive paragraph here:

My favorite toy is

Reading Lesson 13

Student Version

K. Writing Practice

Show Feelings. Beginning writers will tell their reader someone is sad or happy, angry or excited rather than showing the reader the emotions of the character. It is far more powerful to paint a picture of a character's inner state of being by writing about their pacing, their shouts of joy, or the expression they are wearing on their face. Many other fascinating details are possible!

Tell	Mr. Martin was sad.
Show	As he entered the classroom, the students saw their favorite teacher had changed overnight. He no longer looked at them but stared out the window. He lifted his heavy backpack to the desk like it was filled with bricks. Without a smile, he moved ever so slowly to the chalkboard.

Draw a picture of the Mr. Martin the author **shows** us.

Reading Lesson 13   Student Version

K. Writing Practice

Directions: Read each paragraph, then circle the adjective in the list that best describes how the person feels.

1) Caroline arrived breathlessly fifteen minutes early and walked quickly around the room, darting here and there aimlessly. Glancing every other minute at the clock, she bit her fingernails.

late   sad   nervous

2) Enrique sang in the shower. Then he danced around as he dried himself off, and whistled as he carefully put on his expensive new white tuxedo.

nervous   excited   cold

Draw a picture of one of these characters.

Reading Lesson 13

Student Version

K. Writing Practice

Paint a picture. Often beginning writers tell a reader something was "pretty" or "nice" rather than showing the reader a "painting" of the sight. They make the mistake of NOT putting themselves in the reader's shoes. Readers love a good story. But if all you do is write that a sight was "lovely" the reader won't be able to see it. The following exercise may help you paint a picture for your reader.

Tell	The lake was pretty.
Show	The lake was so deep it didn't reflect the color of the light blue sky. In the middle of the lake, a little mountain rose steeply out of the water. On top were old pine trees. The lake was cradled by rock walls covered with snow.

Use your imagination and **show** your readers a painting of the trip to the ocean.

Tell	The trip to the ocean was cool!
Show	

Lesson 14

Reading Lesson 14

A. Vowel Teams

Directions: Highlight the vowel team and read each word.

"tion" says /shun/ as in "fiction"

action   motion   potion   hesitation
nation   option   lotion   notion
station fiction caution emotion

"sion" says /shun or zhun/ as in "vision"

mission   tension   erosion   version
session   illusion   decision mansion
incision occasion   revision invasion

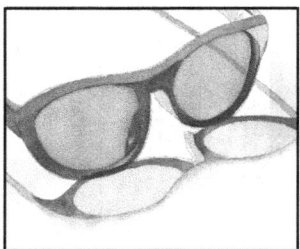

"ar" says /ur/ as in "hangar"

solar   nectar   standard dollar
calendar   lunar   regular   cellar
cheddar   collar   blizzard popular

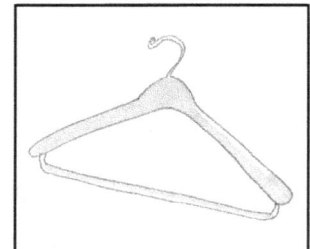

Reading Lesson 14 — Student Version

B. Spelling Practice

Directions: First, highlight the vowel team in each word. Next, write these words in the correct vowel section.

Word List - New Vowel Teams

1. cap<u>tion</u> ✓
2. illu<u>sion</u> ✓
3. nect<u>ar</u> ✓
4. calendar
5. portion
6. mansion
7. confusion
8. station
9. lunar

"tion" says /shun/ as in "fiction"

example: cap<u>tion</u>

"sion" says /zhun/ or /shun/ as in "vision"

example: illu<u>sion</u>

"ar" says /ur/ as in "hangar"

example: nect<u>ar</u>

Reading Lesson 14   Student Version

C. Decoding Practice

**There are four strategies that help us divide words into syllables.
Every syllable must have a vowel.**

Strategy 1:
Dividing Words Into Syllables - Double-same/double-different consonants

Find the two middle consonants and mark a "syllable wall" inside them.
Make sure there is a vowel on either side of the syllable wall.

Example 1 - Double-same	**Example 2 - Double-different**
suf|fix	ad|mit

fossil	option
session	platform
cheddar	nocturnal

Strategy 2:
Dividing Words Into Syllables - Open/closed syllables

When two consonants are not in the middle of a word, do the following:

1) Find the first vowel and put a syllable wall after it. The vowel will say its name. **This is an example of an open syllable.**

2) Make a CVC pattern (Consonant-Vowel-Consonant) and put a syllable wall after it. The vowel will make a short vowel sound. **This is an example of a closed syllable.** (the CVC pattern is highlighted in the example)

Example 1 - Open Syllables	**Example 2 - Closed Syllables**
si|lent	lem|on (CVC)

bacon	vivid
silent	river
human	rapid

Reading Lesson 14　　　　　　　　　　Student Version

C. Decoding Practice

Strategy 3: Compound Words

Formed when two small words are put together to make one new big word.

Directions: Draw a line between these words to make compound words.

sea	dream
shoe	print
day	lace
foot	shell

Directions: Circle the two words that make up each compound word.

1. m o t o r c y c l e
2. p l a y g r o u n d
3. s w i m s u i t
4. e y e g l a s s e s

Directions: Use the words in the box to form compound words with "board" and "print."

chalk	foot	finger	surf
key	skate	hand	news

board　　　　　　　　　　　　**print**

_____ board　　　　_____ print

_____ board　　　　_____ print

_____ board　　　　_____ print

_____ board　　　　_____ print

Intermediate Reading

Reading Lesson 14

Student Version

C. Decoding Practice

Strategy 4: Prefixes and Suffixes

Directions: Add "dis," "non," and "un" to each word. Then write the new word. **Example: add "un" to "fair" to make the work "unfair"**

1. _____ appear _____

2. _____ stop _____

3. _____ tie _____

4. _____ fat _____

5. _____ agree _____

Directions: Use the words you created to complete each sentences.
Example: Sometimes the rules of the game are <u>unfair</u>.

1) Her little sister always tries to _____ her shoes.

2) Mollie worked on her project _____ and finished it.

3) She would often _____ with her parents.

4) Have you ever had _____ milk?

5) As it got dark Tim watched the sun _____ .

Reading Lesson 14   Student Version

D. Sight Words

Directions: Color in the box next to each printed word using the correct color.

black		white	
yellow		blue	
green		brown	

E. Vocabulary

Directions: Read each new word and meaning.

station: a regular stopping place for transports

platform: a level, raised surface for passengers

emotion: a strong feeling, or excitement

tickets: tokens that show a fare has been paid

aboard: get onto a vehicle - a car, ship, train, or plane

F. Passage: Down By The Station

<u>Directions</u>: Read the story and circle the vowel groups from the list.

"<u>tion</u>" as in "fic<u>tion</u>"   "<u>sion</u>" as in "mis<u>sion</u> or illu<u>sion</u>"   "<u>ar</u>" as in "hang<u>ar</u>"

Carly and I looked at the calendar. Today was a special occasion. Mom was taking us to the big city on the train for the very first time. We walked to the station. Lately, the train was becoming more popular. So, when we arrived, the platform was crowded. Many people stood waiting for the train. Mom used dollars to buy our tickets. We made a decision to use caution; Mom made sure we stayed behind the yellow line.

Then Carly and I heard the loud blasts from the horn of the train. We saw its strong, bright light approaching. We were filled with emotion; we were so excited. Finally, the motion of the train slowed. Then the brakes screeched and the train came to a halt. After many people got off, we climbed up the stairs to get aboard. Carly said "This is a great occasion!"

Reading Lesson 14

Student Version

G. Written Response

Directions: Read each question and answer with a complete sentence.

1) What is the name of the writer's sister?

2) Where are they going today?

3) How are they getting there?

4) Is the station busy right now?

Reading Lesson 14

Student Version

H. Vowel Sound Practice

The "tion" sound. Read these "tion" words, then draw a picture for each in the empty box.

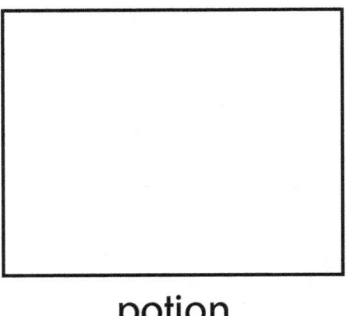

potion

fiction

action

The "sion" sound. Write "sion" to complete each word, then write the whole word.

mis

ses

revi

ver

The "ar" sound. Draw a circle around the words with the "ar" pattern.

| oven | hangar | behind | blizzard | snowy |
| lunar | rainfall | popular | tornado | solar |

page 178

Startup Learning

Reading Lesson 14

Student Version

I. Spelling Practice

"tion" as in "fiction"
Write three words with "tion" in them.

"sion" as in "mansion"
Draw a mansion in the box. Then write three words with "sion" in them.

"ar" as in "hangar"
Draw an hangar in the box. Then write three words with "ar" in them.

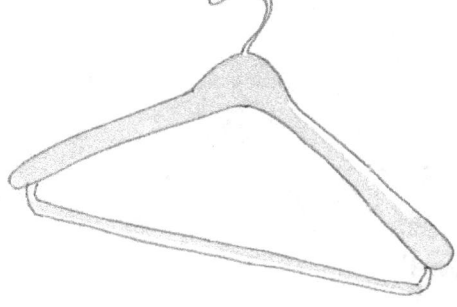

Intermediate Reading

Reading Lesson 14

J. Writing Poetry

Good poetry is able to inspire or delight us depending on the meaning it holds for us. Memorizing a favorite poem is an enjoyable and worthwhile thing to do.

• Have you ever written a poem? _____

• Do you have a favorite poem? _____

• Do you think all poems should rhyme? _____

Let's practice. What rhymes with the following?

1) cat

2) spy

3) bake

4) hook

5) night

6) rocket

7) well

8) time

Reading Lesson 14

Student Version

J. Writing Poetry

Here are some examples of **Light Verse**, poetry that combines whimsy and rhyme. Please notice that each line is one thought. This is not written like a paragraph at all! Also, the ending word in a line often rhymes with the one before it or two lines before it. In addition, poems have a nice meter, rhythm, flow, and beat to them.

Growing
by Mary Ann Hoberman

The grown ups say
  I'm growing tall
And that my clothes
  are growing small.
Can clothes grow small?
I always think
That things grow big
Or else they shrink.
But did they shrink
Or did I grow
Or did we both change?
I don't know.

Pick Up Your Room
by Mary Ann Hoberman

Pick up your room, my mother says
(She says it every day):
My room's too heavy to pick up
(That's what I always say),

Waiters
by Mary Ann Hoberman

Dining with his older daugher
Dad forgot to order water.
Daughter quickly called the waiter
Waiter said he'd bring it later.
So she waited, did the daughter,
Till the waiter brought the water.
When he poured it for her later,
Which one would you call
the waiter?

Rabbit
by Mary Ann Hoberman

  A rabbit
      Bit
  A little bit
  An itty-bitty
    Little bit of beef
  Then bit
    By bit
    He bit
Because he liked the taste of it

Intermediate Reading

Reading Lesson 14

J. Writing Poetry

About the Teeth of Sharks
by John Ciardi

*The thing about sharks is - teeth,
One row above, one row beneath.*

*Now take a closer look. Do you find
It has another row behind?*

*Still closer - here, I'll hold your hat:
Has it a third row behind that?*

*Now look in and... Look out! Oh my,
I'll <u>never</u> now now! Well, goodbye.*

Taking Violin as School
by April Wayland

*I open my case
tighten my bow
pluck a string to tune.
I love to listen to it chirp across
  the echoing room.*

*My friends are in class
reading about
a famous English king.
But I am training this wooden bird
  upon my arm to sing.*

I Eat My Peas with Honey
by Anonymous

*I eat my peas with honey;
I've done it all my life
It makes the peas taste funny,
But it keeps them on the knife.*

I'm Glad I'm Me
by Phil Bolsta

*I don't understand
  why everyone stares
When I take off my clothes
  and dance down the stairs.
Or when I stick carrots
  in both of my ears,
then dye my hair green
  and go shopping at Sears.
I just love to dress up
  and do goofy things.
If I were an angel,
  I'd tie-dye my wings!*

*Why can't folks accept me
  the way that I am?
So what if I'm different
  and don't act like them?
I'm not going to change
  and be someone I'm not.
I like who I am,
  and I'm all that I've got!*

Reading Lesson 14

Student Version

J. Writing Poetry

Choose a topic for your poems from your life. The topic could be a toaster or pet, a car, tree, baseball, the cafeteria, or recess, dinner or your dad, skateboarding or surfing, clothes or shoes or something you love. It could be birthdays or holidays, animals, robots, monsters, toys or iPhones. **Illustrate your poem in the box.**

Intermediate Reading

Lesson 15

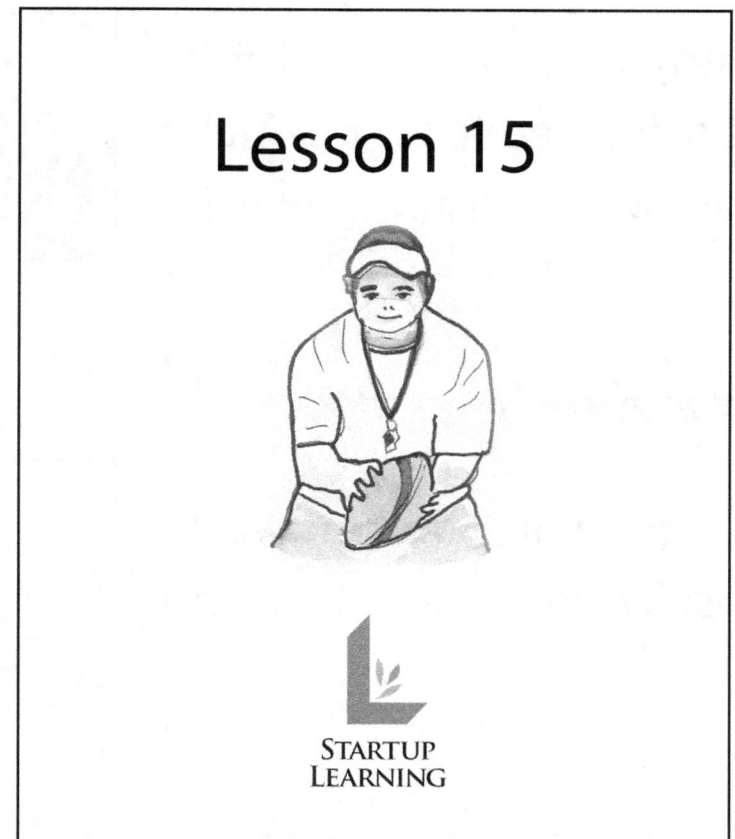

Reading Lesson 15

A. Vowel Teams

Directions: Highlight the vowel team and read each word.

"or" says /er/ as in "harbor"

inventor   mayor   labor   sculptor
conductor doctor editor instructor
professor author senator governor

"or" says /er/ as in "world"

worthy   teamwork worm   work
crossword silkworm word   worth

"ar, arr, er, err" says /air/ as in "parrot"

very   narrow   marry   parent
carry   carrots arid   area
terrace sheriff merry   errand

Reading Lesson 15 — Student Version

B. Spelling Practice

Directions: First, highlight the vowel team in each word. Next, write these words in the correct vowel section.

Word List - New Vowel Teams

1. doct<u>or</u> ✓
2. w<u>or</u>m ✓
3. c<u>arr</u>ot ✓
4. worldly
5. escalator
6. visitor
7. scary
8. silkworm
9. arrow
10. berry

"or" says /er/ as in "harbor"

example: doct<u>or</u>

"or" says /er/ as in "world"

example: w<u>or</u>m

"ar," "arr," "er," "err" says /air/ as in "parrot"

example: c<u>arr</u>ot

Reading Lesson 15

Student Version

C. Decoding Practice

Strategy 1:
Dividing Words Into Syllables - Double-same/double-different consonants

Find the two middle consonants and mark a "syllable wall" inside them. Make sure there is a vowel on either side of the syllable wall.

Example 1 - Double-same
suf|fix

Example 2 - Double-different
ad|mit

shallow
message
babble

cactus
blanket
tractor

Strategy 2:
Dividing Words Into Syllables - Open/closed syllables

When two consonants are not in the middle of a word, do the following:

1) Put a syllable wall after the first vowel. Sound it out to see if it makes a long vowel sound. **This is an open syllable.**

2) If the open syllable doesn't sound like a word, look at the vowel between the two consonants and make a CVC pattern. Then add the syllable wall. **This is a closed syllable.**

Example 1 - Open Syllables
si|lent

Example 2 - Closed Syllables
plan|et

even
bonus
moment

pedals
metal
driven

Reading Lesson 15

Student Version

C. Decoding Practice

Strategy 3: Compound Words

Formed when two small words are put together to make one new big word.

Directions: Draw a line between these words to make compound words.

honey	ship
super	worm
friend	man
earth	bee

Directions: Circle the two words that make up each compound word.

1. n e w s p a p e r
2. h a i r b r u s h
3. w i t h i n
4. l u n c h b o x

Directions: Use the words in the box to form compound words with "berry" and "fall."

| rasp | night | rain | wind |
| blue | out | black | straw |

berry   **fall**

_____ berry   _____ fall

_____ berry   _____ fall

_____ berry   fall _____

_____ berry   _____ fall

Intermediate Reading

C. Decoding Practice

Strategy 4: Prefixes and Suffixes

Directions: Circle the best answer for each question.

1) A **prefix** is part of a word attached to:
   a) the middle of a base word
   b) the beginning of a base word
   c) the end of a base word

2) What is the meaning of the word **reappear**?
   a) appear again
   b) does not appear
   c) someone who appears

3) What is the meaning of the word **inventor**?
   a) before inventing
   b) without inventing
   c) a person who invents things

4) What is the meaning of the word **skillful**?
   a) has skills
   b) before skills
   c) a person who has skills

5) A **suffix** is part of a word attached to:
   a) the middle of a base word
   b) the beginning of a base word
   c) the end of a base word

Reading Lesson 15

Student Version

D. Vocabulary

Directions: Choose a word from the box and write it below the correct picture.

| instructor | senator | doctor | sheriff | sculptor |
| conductor | author | illustrator | inventor | |

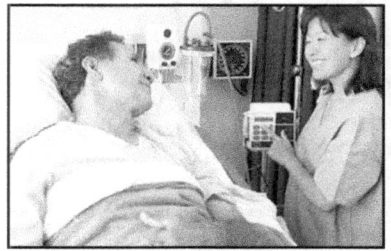

Intermediate Reading

Reading Lesson 15

E. Passage: The World of Work

CCSS.ELA-LITERACY.RF.2.4

Directions: Read the story and circle the vowel teams from the list.

"<u>or</u>" as in "harb<u>or</u>"   "<u>ar, arr, er, err</u>" as in "p<u>ar</u>rot"   "<u>or</u>" as in "w<u>or</u>ld"

There are many interesting jobs in this world. A person can be an instructor teaching at a school. Or they can be a professor teaching at a college. An unusual job is working on a train as a conductor. If a person is musical, they can be a conductor leading an orchestra. A person working in a hospital or clinic can be a doctor. Or if a person is interested in keeping the law, they can be a sheriff.

If a person is political, they can be a mayor of a town, or a senator or governor of a state. A person who likes writing can work as an author or editor. And a person who likes art can be an illustrator or sculptor. Finally, another great area of labor is to discover new ways of doing things by being an inventor.

Reading Lesson 15 Student Version

F. Written Response

Directions: Read each question and answer with a complete sentence.

1) What are two jobs in teaching?

2) What does a conductor do?

3) Where can a doctor work?

4) What does an inventor do?

Reading Lesson 15

G. Vowel Sound Practice

The "or" sound. Read these "or" words, then draw a picture for each in the empty box.

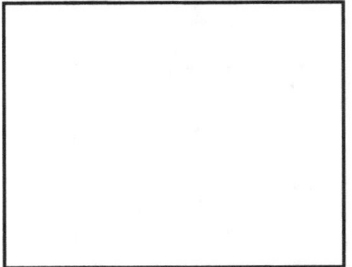
motor

harbor

alligator

The "or" sound. Write "or" to complete each word, then write the whole word.

w_____kload

crossw_____d

w_____thy

silkw_____m

The "ar, arr, er, err" sound. Draw a circle around the words with these pattern.

very	arid	plenty	terrace	parent
cheeses	merry	narrow	beets	peas

Reading Lesson 15

Student Version

H. Spelling Practice

"or" as in "harbor"

Draw a harbor scene in the box. Then write three words with "or" in them.

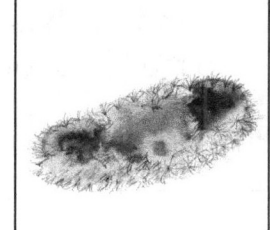

"or" as in "silkworm"

Write three words with "or" in them.

"arr" as in "carrot"

Draw a carrot in the box. Then write three words with "ar, arr, er, or err" in them.

Intermediate Reading

Reading Lesson 15

I. Haiku

Haikus are short poems that are usually written in three lines. The first line has five syllables, the second line has seven and the last has five. Haikus try to capture an image or a feeling about nature or a beautiful experience.

Here are some examples of Haiku.

An afternoon breeze expels cold air, along with the fallen brown leaves.	Orange, yellow, red. Leaves dance as the wind blows strong. They fall to the ground.
Cherry blossoms bloom, softly falling from the tree, explode into night.	The warmth on my skin. Fire falls beneath the trees. I see the sun set.
Summer here again. Music plays sweetly, drifting. And life is renewed.	Love is like winter Warm breaths thaw cold hearts until one day the spring comes.

Reading Lesson 15 — Student Version

I. Haiku

Now, you can try writing some Haikus.

Congratulations

You have completed the Startup Learning

Intermediate Reading Course

_____

Student Name

_____

Teacher Name

www.ingramcontent.com/pod-product-compliance
Lightning Source LLC
Chambersburg PA
CBHW081743100526
44592CB00015B/2280